D1420979

DEAR McSWEENEY'S

McSWEENEY'S
SAN FRANCISCO

Cover illustration by Pieter Van Eenoge

ISBN: 978-1-952119-01-9

10 9 8 7 6 5 4 3 2 1

www.mcsweeneys.net

Printed in the United States

DEAR McSWEENEY'S

TWO DECADES *of* LETTERS TO THE
EDITOR *from* WRITERS, READERS, *and the*
OCCASIONAL BEWILDERED CONSUMER

Edited by DANIEL LEVIN BECKER

CONTENTS

CONTENTS

CONTENTS

EDITOR'S NOTE

The letters gathered here are letters to the editor, right? According to the letter of the law, yes. But the spirit—that's tricky. They do not, for the most part, do the things we ordinarily expect reader mail to accomplish: they don't respond to work run in previous issues of *McSweeney's Quarterly*, or correct errors made therein, or air dissenting views on proposed legislation. For the most part they are unpredictable snapshots and slices of life, domestic tableaux and dispatches from abroad, libertine anecdotes and obsessive mini-essays and epistles into the void that aspire, madly, beautifully, to a communal experience of fleeting momentousness. They were invited or commissioned or unsolicited; they are true, or not entirely true, or not remotely. They are as various as their authors and as formally untidy as life itself. I cannot say with certainty, by the way, that all of their authors actually exist.

And still, they all begin the same way. DEAR MCSWEENEY'S, over and over, page after page, year after year for twenty-three years, a mantra punctuated only by the occasional DEAR EDITOR and in one case a DEAR SIRS. I find something oddly reassuring in this repetition, a warming glow of familiarity even though I personally was never the editor to which they were addressed. They weren't written to me, I mean, but here they are telling me things anyway, taking me into their improbable confidences through the thin scrim of a magazine's name. They'll take you in, too, if you keep reading. We are all MCSWEENEY'S, not to get grandiose or anything.

If these letters accomplish one thing consistently, I think it's this: they record the moments in which readers talk themselves into becoming writers. Many of them were writers already, of course, even the possibly fictitious ones—but I think to be a writer, if you're doing it properly, is to become one incessantly. Out loud, in private, in the margins or in the woods. To learn again and again, thanks to a passage in Thoreau or a spiritual encounter with a Junior Mint, that the world in its serenity and grandeur is there to be noticed and captured and shared. We don't choose where that magic comes from any more than we choose where it winds up, but making space for it in the front of a magazine seems to me the least we can do.

DANIEL LEVIN BECKER
PARIS, FRANCE

PREFACE

The main thing about a letter to McSweeney's is that it begins with DEAR MCSWEENEY'S, and that it should be easy. I mean, of course, not too difficult, but I also mean natural, uncontrived—whatever happens to be on the letter-writer's mind. It is different from a social media post in that those are all about distraction, and these come from a place of concentration. The letters are creative pieces, but not ones that have been subjected to all these high expectations that writers have for themselves: that it be set in scene, that each line be incandescent, that it advance the plot, whatever their particular training/taste/mood/masochism suggests.

All this, to me, feels like it doesn't need saying, but I have two friends—my husband and April, a writer who lives in Virginia, I think—and both of them, when I mentioned this introduction, asked me what a letter to McSweeney's is. So: it is like that. It is like a letter to a pen pal, or a love letter to an imaginary thing. When I say "love letter" I mean it in the contemporary sense. That is, not an actual piece of paper with actual writing, but a text message sent, while standing in line at the airport, to a person who isn't there. "I'm standing in line at the airport. This guy in front of me just gave the ticket agent the finger." Are you with me? I'm saying there is that part of loving someone that takes place when they are not there, and you're experiencing your mundane situation lit up by their imaginary presence, and so you want to describe your situation to them in words.

I have said all that I can say about these letters.

My tooth enamel is thin. I was in high school when I had my first root canal. I had a strong reaction to the nitrous oxide. I was relatively innocent—no drug experimentation, no boys—but responded to the nitrous oxide like a seasoned addict. I understood that I needed the nurse to turn the nitrous oxide up, and that to get her to do that I needed to pretend to feel pain. So that is what I did. She started to make faces, to express confusion, but she trusted me, and so she kept saying, "Does this hurt? Are you sure you're not feeling pressure?" and then dialing up the nitrous. When my dentist came in, she said, "What's the weather like out there?" I was so high that I thought she was making an unusually witty remark. I thought she was commenting on my having left her realm and entered another realm. "What's the weather like in the realm of flying-high-on-nitrous?" I was too high to respond, so I just sort of half laughed, half made a noise. She was confused, and repeated the question. I waved a hand, like stop, stop, it's too much. She put a hand on my forearm and spoke slowly, "Amie? Is it hot outside?" "Oh," I said. "Yes." She bent over and cranked my nitrous dial down, and I was unhappy.

This is not what I wanted to talk about. I wanted us to finally get honest about my teeth. I broke my first tooth at around twenty-seven, on a piece of microwave popcorn. I was living in my office at *The Onion*. This is another digression. I had been living in a brownstone in South Park Slope. I had the entire second floor. The apartment was a one-bedroom with a claw-foot tub, and it cost $800 a month. It was below market value, but my landlady lived below me, on the first floor. I guess she was a good person... No. You know what? She was grotesque. She went around in a torn nightgown and had a lot of plastic, battery-operated seasonal decor. At night she would let herself into my apartment. I woke up several times with her standing over my bed, saying, "Amie, the leak!"

I was not happy, but I had no plans to leave. Then, one month, I slid the rent in cash under her door, as I did every month, and she told me she never got it. So I was evicted. Of course I could've made some case about it, but I wasn't happy.

I rented a different apartment. I had one month between apartments with nowhere to live, and so I was living on a cot in my office at *The Onion*. I broke a tooth on a piece of microwave popcorn, so I searched for "dentist" online, and that is how I ended up in a carpeted basement, having the gum below my broken tooth lanced by a flirtatious man in a leather coat. He gave me a prescription for a hundred Vicodin, most of which I gave to a coworker. I'm as reckless as the next guy, but I just couldn't lie on a cot in my office and form an opioid addiction.

You know, it occurs to me that I also lived in the store at *McSweeney's*. I had no intention of bringing that up. It was the year 2000. Let's not dwell on it.

Taipei, 2013. I had a toothache that developed into a fever with an abscess. I tried to find a dentist, but I was having difficulty with the language barrier and culture clash. I am a tall woman. In Taipei, I think, I am what you might call an ogre. So the people of Taipei were disgusted and confused when I spoke to them. I had friends there, but they didn't really understand that the situation was serious. You say "toothache" and people don't really imagine that they are speaking to someone with horrible, horrible, horrible teeth. The infection had entered my bone, and could have caused a lot of trouble if it were not for my mother. She was in Taipei, too. Despite my having abandoned her in Tokyo days before (another digression, does not reflect well on me, so given the whole accidental live-at-work pileup let's skip it) she went out and hit the pavement. She went from store to store in Taipei, asking for amoxycillin. Taipei is not like Mexico in the nineties. The people of Taipei are more rulebound than the people of America, plus there was the ogre factor. Can you imagine going into a CVS in America and asking for antibiotics? It would not work. There were all the barriers I have described, but my mom did get antibiotics, and I took them, and everything was fine.

I have another tooth story, but I get the feeling we're kind of running out of tooth story juice, and can I just say I feel better? I'm so glad we're finally being honest.

AMIE BARRODALE
KANSAS CITY, MO

DEAR MCSWEENEY'S,

Welcome to your twenties. I passed mine much the way you have been so far, carried the same kind of broken furniture up and down flights of stairs, had the same assortment of roommates, the same old appliances that can't be cleaned, though, like you, I cleaned the hell out of them. I had similar half solutions and about a hundred jobs. I groped.

It is the decade for that. High school is over. College, for those who go, ends. There is no further official sanctioned path for you. You are spit out of the system, tasked with supporting yourself (good luck), and must endure all the tautological admonishments to "be yourself." For the first time, you are utterly undetermined.

Here's a story. One night at the beginning of my twenties, I was walking to my apartment from the train and came upon a strange structure, a giant apparatus of pulleys and ladders and wire. It had somehow unraveled in front of my building. It stretched for half a block, rose two stories high, and was lit up like a vast construction site. As I moved closer, I could see people crawling around on it. They were up on a scaffolding; they were turning large wheels. Not construction workers. *Angels*, in white robes, with feathery wings and large eyes, some of their faces so white they seemed chalked; others, very dark.

It was not a vision, McSweeney's. It was an art installation. Someone had come along and put it there to confuse us.

I noticed a herd of people lined up beside it. The head angel was collecting forms people had filled out. She was taking the slips of paper and attaching them one by one to a wire. The forms then rode through the maze on the wire, around corners, up to the top, where the final angel stood on a precarious platform, her robes and wings very pale against the dark. She tied each slip of paper to a balloon. Then she lifted to her toes and let the balloon drift into the sky.

The sound of peaceful strumming, a soft wind.

The people around me were gazing up. We were dull, rumpled, washed-out as a newspaper. We watched the slips of paper disappear into the night and we were all wondering the same thing: could it be so easy to float away what we don't want?

We'd fucked up so much, we were thinking. We wanted to move forward, but our flaws held us back.

I hurried to the table and took a form. I scrawled a shape on it that only I and whoever could see into my mind could understand. But it contained all I needed it to.

I was the last one in that long, long line. The line was so long that by the time I reached the front, it was midnight, and the angels in the sky were stepping down off their suspended chairs. They were leaving! I reached out my trembling hand to the head angel, but she said "You're too late" in a nasal voice—in English, though a moment before she'd spoken only angel language.

Too late? The strumming stopped and all I could hear was a cold, harsh, howling wind.

I'll tell you what I did, McSweeney's. I shoved my form into her hand anyway. I thought she might throw it back at me in a wadded ball and take off running, but she didn't. She groused a little, stomped off and got a balloon, tied it, and let it go, making a mean face at me as she did.

It didn't go gently, McSweeney's. It careened haphazardly and too fast. I thought it might get stuck in a tree, but it continued upward. That paper left this earth.

But I hadn't seen the last of it, as I'd believed. I thought we were floating those papers up into the sky to get rid of what was on them. But I was wrong. We were sending out pieces of ourselves, like an advance team, into the universe.

HERE I AM.

HERE I AM.
HERE I AM.

HERE I AM.

HERE I AM.

HERE I AM.
HERE I AM.
HERE I AM.

I know this because that scrawl pulled me up with it. I felt my feet slowly lifting and following. It pulled me through twenty-two, twenty-three, thirty, like a rope dropped into the fire, raising me out of the volcano and on into the future. That scrawl turned out to be my strength, not my weakness.

Here you are, McSweeney's, scrawl and all. It's you. Vibrant, startling, light-filled. Headed toward the sky. Lifted by angels and air. You, advancing.

Love,

DEB OLIN UNFERTH
AUSTIN, TX

from ISSUE 12

DEAR MCSWEENEY'S,

I would like to tell you about the moths in my studio. They are called miller's moths. They appear to belong to the order Lepidoptera. Beyond these pieces of recalled knowledge I can provide only my observations.

The moths are brownish-gray but sometimes slightly paler after they die. They are attracted to burning light bulbs but do not usually sit on them and burn up as the white moths of my childhood did. When there is no strong light, these "millers" whip themselves about the room and beat themselves to death against the walls. I am guessing this is how they die and why, every morning, I must vacuum the carpet of moths before I begin work. But I do not see them hit the wall and fall to the floor, so perhaps they come in at night only in order to die quietly inside a room, among their own.

Often when I wake up in the house and throw off the bedclothes, a piece of a wing or a segment of exoskeleton wafts ceilingward on the updraft. In fact, most nights I sleep with a moth or moths. Before falling asleep I thrash in my bed if I feel the telltale stroke of wings against an arm or a leg and, in my lethargy, assume my thrashing body will free the moths from my nest. Probably I crush them to death.

I would use the glass sliding door that leads from my room to the outside if hundreds of moths did not live in the narrow flat space between the screen and the glass. When I move the inner glass door at all, the moths rise up as one in a terrifying, shape-shifting cloud of gray and brown wings. The sound of all their bodies hitting the metal screen and glass panel at the same time is hideous.

One frequently flies up my pant leg while I sit at my desk, and I swear and hit at myself as if the moth has entered my very body, until it emerges from my clothing alive or dead. If it flies out I try to swat it to the ground and grind it under my foot. This practice leaves dusty marks under the desk in no regular pattern.

When one of the moths bats against a windowpane from the inside, sometimes a bird flies into the glass to take it. It is disheartening to watch a bird's repeated attempts to take the moth until it is too exhausted to further attempt flying through the glass. These birds, perhaps even the same ones, have stopped attaching their mud-daubed nests to the top of the house since several plastic owls have been hung from the gutters. The owls swing back and forth in the breeze as if from gallows-poles.

The moths have six legs: two long, thin ones joining the body at its middle; two large, thick ones emerging from the top of the body; and two smaller ones from the middle of the thorax. The body is segmented, with eight segments below the thorax, which is slightly redder in color than the rest of the body. The head is dark brown and has two antennae.

The wings number four: two large back wings and two smaller ones nearer the head. When the moth is at rest, the wings lie in two layers. The upper wings are darker, especially at the ends, which are tipped in hundreds of tiny feathery hairs. The larger wings underneath are a silvery taupe and open like fans when the upper wings are stretched to the sides as if in flight. When smeared on a sheet of white paper, the wing dust looks gold.

The body looks as if covered with fine down, and when stroked it feels soft as a pussy willow. With the slightest pressure, pincerlike structures emerge from the body's lower tip. The pincers are covered in the same down.

The head is the darkest part of the moth. At the tip are two fuzzy pincers or teeth. The antennae are about three-eighths of an inch long and have the thickness of human hairs, growing thinner toward the tips.

Oh every girl that ever I've touched, I did not do it harmfully. I listen to music as I write and swat moths. Sometimes the lyrics make me think of something, as of how each young man in each town in this country, from the very beginning of the settlement of this continent, let alone every young man of every village in human history, loved a girl or a few girls he met in his village or somewhere else, and how each man's whole world was his work, and those girls, and the dreams he was delivered in his sleep by a cruel or compassionate God. The amount of recollected emotion that disappears from human memory when someone dies, and the degree to which we rely on a few people to record something of what emotions were to them, is almost too much to bear.

Tonight I vacuumed forty-two moths.

Sincerely,

SARAH MANGUSO
SHERIDAN, WY

DEAR MCSWEENEY'S,

I'm a little hung over, so I'll make it short. I've recently moved from Cherokee Nation in Oklahoma to New Mexico, which has a much more salutary climate. Plus, I have yet to see an armadillo out here, thankfully. In Oklahoma I had a few bad experiences with armadillos who managed to get into my garage from time to time and pervaded the air with fear and paranoia. It was unsettling, to say the least.

The last armadillo I saw before I moved was the most disturbing of them all. I skipped work that day to stay home and celebrate the paperback release of my latest novel and have a nice smoke and listen to Ornette Coleman's *Friends and Neighbors: Live at Prince Street* on vinyl. What a fantastic album. What a fantastic day.

Then things turned. I remember I was eating a popsicle and reading an article about how cows' tongues manufacture an antibiotic that aids in healing wounds, when I heard something knocking around in the garage.

I was pretty sure it was another armadillo, so I was careful when I lifted the garage door and entered. Right away I saw the little fucker in the corner. Armadillos are usually costive and non-menacing, but I immediately sensed this one's hubris.

It looked directly at me. I would've called the city for help, as I had done in the past, but then, still looking me in the eyes, it showed its teeth and hissed. I took umbrage at this: how dare this armadillo have the cojones to enter my garage and look directly at me in such a threatening way?

Despite me waving my arms and clapping, it wouldn't run out, so I picked up a shovel and slowly approached it. (Let me just say I had no intention of killing it or hurting it at this point. I'm not great with any kind of rodents, especially ones that carry leprosy—yes, armadillos carry leprosy—so you can imagine how nervous I was. I merely wanted to chase it out of the garage.)

The weed I'd smoked was starting to kick in. I wear Native American jewelry, and the sun coming in reflected off one of my necklaces and onto the armadillo, which made it hiss at me again.

Ever hear the terrifying hiss of an armadillo?

Here's where things really get strange. The armadillo opened its mouth and hissed these words: "I'm Andrew Jackson, seventh president of the United States."

It smiled, showing teeth.

What is one supposed to do with such astringent information? More important: What kind of fool is Andrew Jackson to admit this to a Cherokee Nation citizen?

Fuck him. I approached him and swung the shovel with my eyes closed, but he managed to run past me out of the garage. I saw him scurry into the bushes by the side of the house.

I took my cell phone out and dialed my wife: "Armadillo in our bushes!"

"Call animal control," she told me.

"It's Andrew Jackson in the body of an armadillo," I told her. "I've caught him. He's in our bushes. I can hear him chewing and snorting around in there, the little fucker."

"If it's Andrew Jackson," she said, "you have my permission to beat him to death."

I hung up and poked the bushes with the shovel. I kept hearing the plangent sound of his snort—it was so strange, whatever he was doing in the bushes. I was taut with anxiety. Do armadillos spit? It seemed like I'd heard that somewhere. This made me more worried about his leprosy.

The leprosy, the leprosy. Killing Andrew Jackson with a shovel would likely spread blood and leprosy. What could I do?

I sat on the driveway for a long time, thinking about it. Here he was, Andrew Jackson, seventh president of the United States. I thought about all the brutal and egregious shit he did during his term. I thought about my ancestors and the thousands of people he forced from their land. I thought about the wounded, the sick, the ones who died on the Trail of Tears. And now I had him here. What better vengeance was there than to make him suffer a slow death?

My friends: let it be known that I did not kill Andrew Jackson.

Let it be known that I gathered all my strength and yelled, swatting at the bushes with my shovel, until Andrew Jackson ran out. I chased him then.

I chased him while swinging the shovel and screaming like a goddamn lunatic. I chased him westward, westward, just as he had chased my ancestors from their land.

Let it be known that I chased Andrew Jackson through the field beside my house. I chased him all the way out to I-35, where cars flew by, headed south in heavy traffic, and I watched him run into it.

May wolves and beasts unite in venery!

Wado,

BRANDON HOBSON
LAS CRUCES, NM

from ISSUE 38

DEAR MCSWEENEY'S,

A few years ago, I read an interview with Helen Hunt. It was only an okay interview, but she shared her grandmother's coconut macaroon recipe, which I've been meaning to try ever since. I can't remember if the interview was in your publication or in *Redbook*. Can you look into this and let me know? Thanks so much,

JEN STATSKY
NEW YORK, NY

DEAR MCSWEENEY'S,

Have you ever confessed that you like Michael Crichton, only to receive one of those knowing grins, as if by saying you like Michael Crichton you really mean that you don't like Michael Crichton, when in fact you couldn't be clearer?

Maybe it's just me. And maybe the skepticism is understandable, even warranted. After all, Crichton's characters usually have less depth than his jacket embossings. He describes the human heart like a befuddled parent explaining how an air conditioner works to a small child. His climate-change naysaying is a regrettable coda to a career spent dramatizing the unforeseen consequences of technological progress. But when he's on his game, he achieves the near impossible, crafting techno-thrillers so momentous they zoom right past their shortcomings.

Let me backtrack. I first crossed paths with the Crichtonian oeuvre one summer when I worked as a caddy. I must have been fifteen or sixteen years old. I'd never before been in a country club, or on a golf course, but the caddy master—seriously, that was the title on his business cards—wasn't particularly eagle-eyed. Each morning I arrived to the caddy shack, put my name on the daily sign-up sheet, and waited around for five hours or so, until my name was called out from a tinny speaker that rattled like a can of loose change when the caddy master spoke. Those long stretches of morning went infinitely quicker with M.C. for company.

That summer I tore through *Congo*, *The Andromeda Strain*, *Terminal Man*, *Sphere*, *Jurassic Park*, *The Lost World*, *The Great Train Robbery*, *Eaters of the Dead*, *Rising Sun*, and *Airframe*. Until then, my extracurricular reading life generally consisted of R. L. Stine's *Fear Street* series. Crichton's ecotone, wherein genius met hubris, was significantly more frightening than stories of ski trips with overprivileged, underparented high school students (viz. *Ski Weekend, Fear Street No. 10*). The urgent need to know what would happen next kept me sneaking pages on the fairways and reading long into the night.

Recently I re-reread *Timeline*, one of Crichton's deep cuts (if a writer who could sell the film rights to his shopping list can be said to have deep cuts). It tells the story of a few modern-day medievalists sent back to a fourteenth-century French town in a parallel universe. Their universe-hopping time machine breaks down, but luckily the medievalists are hip to four-teenth-century customs. Plus they have sweet sword fighting skills. Meanwhile in the present, their colleagues joust with a tech company in boardroom battles that neatly echo the brutality of court politics. Spoiler alert: their billion-dollar technology wasn't developed solely to expand our understanding of Franco-Plantagenet relations. Instead, there's a CEO two hounds shy of being Montgomery Burns with hidden plans for time-travel adventure tourism (guess he hasn't read *Jurassic Park*).

Like Crichton's best work, it's a modern-day *Frankenstein*. It takes the heady predicament of an invention outgrowing the inventor's capacity for moral wisdom, and serves it up with crowd-pleasing panache. Its architecture is as meticulously crafted as the Gothic cathedrals populating its pages, and those pages turn with forceful velocity.

Michael Crichton's books were the starting point for me as an adult reader, the first substantial forays into literature's multiverse. Without them I may not have pursued reading far enough down the rabbit hole to one day look back with genuine affection. A novel doesn't need to be Great to be great. A novel doesn't need to be revolutionary to be life-changing for one reader.

And that reader hopes Michael Crichton is well, in whatever parallel universe he rests.

ANTHONY MARRA
OAKLAND, CA

DEAR MCSWEENEY'S,

Pretend for a moment that you're shopping for a new gas range. In fact, let's imagine you're doing a little kitchen remodel, as people do, and you're going to treat yourself to some new appliances. You and your partner have a long list of features you want or don't want in this new gas range, and you spend a lot of time in awful places like Home Depot and Best Buy twiddling knobs and caring about things like warming drawers. And let's say you finally find one that's perfect—I mean *perfect*—in every way. It has the thing that does the thing, it's got five whatevers, it's adequately shiny, and it has enough BTUs to cook a nice French meal for ten people even though you will mostly use it for making scrambled eggs and "garbagedillas," which are quesadillas made with bits and pieces of leftover food. This range looks fantastic, it's the right size, and it's the right price. Like I said, it's perfect. Except for one thing.

On the console, there is a button that says CHICKEN NUGGETS.

What if that one button, those two words that bring saturated joy into the fatty hearts and minds of so many American children, was so offensive to your culinary sensibilities that you couldn't find any way to overlook it? What if you knew that every time you approached your new cooktop Cadillac, you would see only that button? Or not only that button, but also the button next to it that says PIZZA. What I'm saying is, what if you knew you would clench your jaw, trembling in bathrobed silence there on the new Marmoleum, taunted by your decision to let this button into your home, until you finally exploded with rage and started shouting "This is what's wrong with America!" before stumbling backward to collapse in sorrow, pounding your fists on your reclaimed-fir butcher-block countertops while your wife shook her head and pointed out again that all of this outrage is coming from the same man who is known for bringing Funyuns to social gatherings?

Could you buy that range? Could you live with it? Because I can't. You suck, Frigidaire.

SLOAN SCHANG
PORTLAND, OR

DEAR MCSWEENEY'S,

Whenever I see three question marks in a row, I think about getting divorced. I met my husband, whom I'm now separated from, when I was eighteen and in college. We had our first date a year and a half after we met, at the library, and it was all asking. What's that book you're reading? Why don't you like Burger King? Is that a birthmark? What was it like traveling to South Africa? Is that Randall Cunningham jersey your favorite shirt? I had so many questions, but the beautiful thing was that he did, too! I finally had someone who wanted to really know me. I fell in love with him because he cared deeply about my interior life.

Then, after eight years together, our relationship was suddenly marked by uncertainty. Our questions devolved into a roll call of harried pleading. Why don't you want kids? Will you go to therapy? Will you please go to therapy? Why won't you go with me? Are you cheating on me? Can you give me a year to figure this out? Please? It turned out we hadn't been all the way truthful with our answers, or hadn't asked right, or just changed too quickly. Eventually, the conversations had become one-sided, and the gentle querying turned passive-aggressive. Every question had a sigh or a shrug built into its grammatical structure. We grew and grew until we grew apart, and someone put a period on the whole thing.

That experience has attuned me to the affront of three question marks in a row. We used them in texts and e-mails near the end, and so even when we spoke I heard them in our voices. The consequence of my romance's transformation into a den of emotional hostility is that I now see more than one question mark in a row as the grim reaper's scythes. They recall the doom of "read" receipts, of bed death, of what happens when someone you love gets tired of you. In my mind, triple question marks are an emblem of angst, an emoji of exasperation.

As a collective symbol, three question marks is a signal of impatience, a confusing way to elicit information. Rather than suggesting a hunger for knowledge, as the repetition may appear to imply, they connote chaos, someone jamming a keyboard in frustration. The identical marks bring to mind metastasis. Their curvature is the arc of raised eyebrows, their order the time-lapse of a defeated person, grief and habit hooking the spine into bad posture like mine. Or the smoke curling up from too many blunts. The older folks in my family have a saying: "Death comes in threes." So it was ironic that the communication patterns I'd previously bragged about in my new-age, fifty-fifty relationship eventually affirmed that old-school sentiment.

Of course, three question marks can be fun. My friends know I hate three in a row so they use them to make me laugh. Sometimes three can mean pure bewilderment, or excitement. When you use three question marks at the end of good news, like "We got Markelle Fultz???" they can resemble the fuzzy-wipe effect of an onscreen dream sequence. They are more whimsical than exclamation points and more mysterious than animated icons.

Lynne Truss, that multi-hyphenate writer and commenter on grammar, described an early application of the question mark, *Punctus Interrogativus* of the eighth century, as a "lightning ash, striking from right to left." One question mark no longer looks that way, but three shocks me to my core. In a 2011 article for *Wired* magazine, dating expert Sam Greenspan cataloged several common grammatical symbols as they pertain to text-speech. "Question marks have a tendency to stack onto each other. And with each stack the meaning changes," he writes. For example, "What time do you want to meet up" accompanied by one question mark is "simple, unassuming, and friendly. Gets the point across, elicits a response, but also drives toward a solution." Two "looks like a typo." Three, on the other hand, "feels impatient, childish. It's an aggressive question: It demands a response, and suggests that the response had better be to your liking."

Which brings me to my point. Last week, I finally decided to reenter the dating scene. After months of saying no to this guy who works at my local Ethiopian bakery, I gave him my phone number. We agreed to meet for a drink after his shift ended. Fifteen minutes before the date, he texted to say that something had come up and that he would be twenty minutes late, and did I have time to wait??? Of course I had time to wait. I'd been single for a year and a half. The only thing on my agenda that night was refereeing a literal cat fight that popped off in my kitchen between my roommate's two domestic kitties and her newly adopted street kitten that owns the hallway after dark. But when I saw the blitzkrieg of the three ???s I recoiled and wrote back that I had work in the morning, sorry. I'm afraid I'm unduly traumatized by these signs. Will men think I'm anal-retentive if I explain why I really, really hate seeing such symbols stacked together? Is it too much to reveal when you first meet someone? I'll have to figure this out. Anyway, I just wanted to write a letter of appreciation to you, McSweeney's, for not clotting up your pages with superfluous punctuation. Your grammatical discretion bespeaks an inner strength I find attractive.

Yours,

NIELA ORR
PHILADELPHIA, PA

DEAR MCSWEENEY'S,

Do you know what a twitcher is? Apparently, in bird-watching circles, the term is used to refer to people so beguiled by the spectacle of rare birds that they will actually twitch and tic in rapture. At first I thought this too rare a condition to deserve a name, but then I remembered my friend Rabs. I suspect he's a twitcher and doesn't even know it.

I was twelve years old walking across Anderson's field toward Kmart when I first heard Rabs express an interest in birds. Of course, he wasn't Rabs back then. Then he was Mark Jacobson. It would be another year until he renamed himself to match the white embroidery of a secondhand jacket his mom gave him for Christmas—I doubt Mark ever knew the real "Rabs."

Anyway, that day we were walking to Kmart to steal basketball cards because Rabs collected them. I remember thinking how warm and blue the air was. I also remember looking down at my feet. That's how I saw the bunny. It was tucked away in some thick grass, all curled up in itself. I called Rabs over and he picked it up. The bunny unfolded in his palm like wet origami. It had holes where its eyes used to be, and looking at it lying there so dead on such a perfect day made me sure that everything in life was hopeless. I looked over at Rabs to tell him so, but before I could explain, he hurled that bunny at Mr. Anderson's house. It fell twenty feet short. We kept walking.

"Aren't birds amazing?" Rabs announced near Kmart's entrance. "I mean, we live on Earth and all over there are these things that just hang in the air, and we call them birds. It's so beautiful."

I didn't know this was the start of something, McSweeney's, so I just nodded, unzipped the back pocket on Rabs's backpack, and walked inside.

Sincerely,

TREVOR KOSKI
CHICAGO, IL

DEAR EDITOR,

For a while now, I've been thinking about a literary sort of experiment. Not really an experiment, I suppose, as there's no hypothesis to prove. Maybe it's more of a prank, although that would imply that someone's going to get embarrassed, and I hope that's not the case.

The idea is to write a very short story that looks like one of those homemade posters folks tack up around the neighborhood to advertise sublets or pleas for the return of a lost puppy. For instance, the story might be titled BELOVED FAMILY PET! and have a photocopy picture of a kitten in happier times at the top, but the story wouldn't be about a lost pet at all. It would be about the joy of love, or the sorrow of a bus crash, or the fear of a mummy seeking horrible vengeance. Whatever. Maybe not a mummy. At the bottom there would be a layer of tear-away paper fringe, each piece with my e-mail address.

Next, I'd make copies of this story-disguised-as-cry-for-help and staple them to telephone poles in my neighborhood and elsewhere around the city. Near one of them, perhaps, I could set up camp on a bench, with a sandwich and a Mountain Dew, and watch for a time. Nine out of ten people, I'm sure, would walk right by, certain it was just another poster for a lost pet. Only folks who approached it with genuine concern, specifically to learn more about the lost kitty, would discover, in fact, that it was something else.

Best,

KEVIN GUILFOILE
CHICAGO, IL

DEAR KEVIN,
Why, exactly, do you want to do this?

EDITOR

DEAR EDITOR:

Why? I like the idea of this story existing out in the street, all over the city, pretending to be something else. I like the thought of people reading the story only after they've been tricked into it. I'm curious to know how many people, having fallen for the bait-and-switch, would take the time to write. I'm intrigued by the benign manipulation, luring people into reading short fiction by their concern for a kitten in peril. Will they be relieved to discover that the cat in question is really safe and dry, nesting on a bathrobe I threw carelessly across my bed, or will they be angry?

KEVIN GUILFOILE
CHICAGO, IL

from ISSUE 3

DEAR MCSWEENEY'S,

If you were a mummy, what would you see? Well, if your eyes hadn't been bandaged yet, here's what!

Your oiled body is wrapped tightly in linen bandages coated with resin. Each finger and toe is wrapped separately. Magical amulets, or charms, such as the scarab, which was a special symbol of the afterlife, are tucked into your wrappings. Tiny statues called shabtis are left in the tomb to be servants to your mummy in the afterlife. Tombs also held your favorite possessions.

Your mummy is placed in a coffin that was shaped and painted to look like a person. Then it might get put inside another coffin! Then you would get placed in a tomb. The whole process, from death through burial, took about seventy days. That's almost two and a half months! Whew!

COLLEEN WERTHMANN
NEW YORK, NY

DEAR SIRS:

When Edison invented the incandescent light bulb, he had his people send out a press release. It said, "A Bright Idea Has Been Born." When Watson and Crick discovered the double-helical structure of the DNA molecule, they had their people send out a press release. It said, "DNA Is Tangled Up in YOU." It is this spirit of entrepreneurial invention that has guided the drafting of this letter, which will serve as an official announcement of the creation of the world's first and only Conceptual Art Registry.

The Conceptual Art Registry shares traits with both the double helix and the light bulb. On the one hand, it is complex and self-referential; on the other hand, it has the power to illuminate. It can best be explained as a kind of catalog that collects hundreds, and possibly thousands, of brief descriptions of ideas for conceptual art shows, ideas which will be organized by type and published to the World Wide Web. Artists of all types, working in all media, from all regions of the world, will then be invited to browse the catalog. Should an artist find an idea that appeals to him, he can license it for his own use. The licensing fee will be determined by a simple formula that takes into account the size of an artist's project, the duration the show is designed to run, the independence of an idea (in other words, whether it is to be used on its own or in a combination with other ideas), and an artist's previous reputation. One-time licensing is expected to run between $100 and $500.

This document is the wrong place to describe the contents of the Registry in detail, but the right place to furnish an overview. The Registry will deal with all varieties of artwork, including gallery shows, performance pieces, video installations, sound sculptures, and new-media artwork. Each category will be denoted with a three-letter abbreviation (GAL for gallery shows, PER for performance pieces, VID for video installations, and so on), and each work assigned a three-digit number, thus limiting the number of conceptual pieces in each category to one thousand, which should be sufficient. The only unifying principle behind the works described in the catalog is that they are conceptual: to wit, that they contain some recursive feature, whether self-referential, self-aggrandizing, or self-anni-hilating, that renders them both superior and inferior to more conventional fine art. Take, for example, GAL387, a variation on an ordinary gallery show that reverses the size relationship between the title cards (those anonymous white labels that contain information about the works displayed in the show) and the works themselves. In any show that uses GAL387 as a conceptual foundation, the labels must be at least five feet square, and the works themselves can be no larger than six inches square. The result is both a comic visual shock and a canny commentary on the ways in which attempts to define works of art can be a form of subversion. Alternatively, there is GAL499, in which all paintings are turned to face the wall. In this case, the paintings can be landscapes, abstracts, portraits of historical figures, hyperrealistic scenes of battle, or any other image. The Registry is only responsible for the idea of turning the images toward the wall.

GAL387 and GAL499 are only two of the many gallery-themed conceptual art pieces that will soon be available for licensing in the Registry. One more example will clarify the matter for those who are still hazy: VID089, which is a video installation that consists of twelve monitors set into gallery walls like paintings, complete with frames. Over each monitor, there is a camera, recessed into the wall, and placed behind plate glass but not hidden. The cameras run throughout active gallery hours—in fact, they run only during the active gallery hours. More to the point, the monitor beneath each camera displays precisely what the camera witnessed the previous day, in real time. In other words, the show consists entirely of a record of the previous day's audience's reaction to the show, which itself consisted entirely of a reaction to the previous day's audience's reaction, and so forth. The footage displayed on the monitor on the first day of the show can be of two varieties: either video of an empty room (that would be VID089a) or a video created by gallery employees that mimics the reactions of average gallery patrons (VID089b). Again, the Registry does not stipulate—indeed, it does not care about—the exact size of the monitors, the nature of the frames, or whether or not the images are accompanied by sound. These are questions that can be answered by individual artists after they have licensed the idea. The Registry cares only about furnishing inspiration to artists, and being compensated appropriately.

The Conceptual Art Registry, privately owned and produced, will be administered by a small staff of accountants and auditors. The terms of usage will be governed by a Standard Licensing Agreement, which will also reside on the site and include such essential sections as "Definition," "Usage," and "Payment and Delivery." Finally, it is worth noting that the Conceptual Art Registry is also its first customer: just this morning, the Registry paid itself a generous fee of $500 for the rights to license NEW065, which is a new-media art project described as a "a kind of catalog that collects hundreds, and possibly thousands, of brief descriptions of ideas for conceptual art shows."

Yours,

BEN GREENMAN

FOUNDER AND SOLE PROPRIETOR
CONCEPTUAL ART REGISTRY
WWW.BENGREENMAN.COM

DEAR MCSWEENEY'S,

The guy across the street is an insurance salesman. He cornered me on my driveway soon after we moved in and asked if I had term or life. He's an affable if fearful person. His six-year-old son was at our house one time and explained that we should never go to New York. "Why's that, J—?" "Because you'd get robbed," he said. "But why's that?" "Because they ban guns. You can't bring your gun." That was a cinematic moment; a lens telescoped out my window, across the street, through their brick walls, into the dinnertime kitchen, to see the conversations between father and son. I didn't begrudge the kid, since I could see where he got it from. Fear must have some basis. This was after his father, the insurance seller, firmly and without prompting advised me not to swerve my car to avoid squirrels or groundhogs or whatever, especially, especially if the family is with me. He barrels down on them. There's no way you prioritize that squirrel over your family's health. I took note. I should also park my car facing out, as he does. He's always got the car facing out the street for an efficient getaway, should it be necessary. When I'm reading on the front porch and he comes home, I see his car pass their driveway, gently brake, and then slowly back in.

I haven't talked much to my neighbors on the other side and up a few houses, but I know the husband is being treated for prostate cancer. He waves from his tool-stocked garage sometimes when I drive by. The neighbor behind us, the one with the trampoline, has been dying of brain cancer for two years. When her husband is walking their dog and I come home to find him at the end of my drive, dog on leash two feet ahead of him, a steaming pile of dog shit two feet behind, and he says, "Oh, that, that was someone else's…" I can only shrug and say "Hi, Billy," because what do you do?

A girl from the bus stop had been missing for a few days before we all learned her appendix had burst. The doctors didn't catch it upon her first hospital visit, and she had to go back late that night sallow, pale, limp, and pretty damn close to death's door. She was in intensive care for weeks, her internal organs undermined. All reports were that they didn't expect her to make it. They used those words. But she made it, and when I hear her grandfather ranting at the bus stop about liberals and his guns and who's out to get him, I don't engage. Her mother committed suicide after she was born. Her grandparents take care of her. I don't know why he's so hate-filled, but I know there's more going on than I see.

The latest self-improvement efforts being made by my wife and me involve trying to understand other people better. That, we suspect, will make us less frustrated. We tried a number of things, not too successfully, so this is the newest plan. Our kids are growing up—soon both of them will be in school, all day, somehow. Jesus, I don't know how it happens. I'm a historian who's no good at dealing with time's passage in my own life. I don't want my children to have to justify their own fears and anxieties by pointing to us. I don't want them to have any. But they'll get them from us anyway, and someone else will (if they're lucky) or will not (more likely) wonder where they came from. We can't avoid it unless this self-improvement kicks in soon.

So there's that.

I was writing because when I got home last week I saw a new car parked in the driveway across the street. It was, as is customary, parked facing the street, and in getaway position. I walked inside. My wife was standing in the living room sorting through mail, the sun angling in across the floor. "I see they got a new car over there. Insurance sales must be booming," I said.

She looked at me, looked out the window, and looked back at me. "No," she said, only barely revealing her smile, just enough so I knew that she'd come to understand some essential truth: "That's his parents' car. They're visiting."

I'll be in touch again soon,

BENJAMIN COHEN
CHARLOTTESVILLE, VA

DEAR MCSWEENEY'S,

I am writing to you after returning from the hospital with my ten-year-old son, Magnus.

Last night Magnus told me he had a bump on his hand.

"It's probably a callus," I said, thinking how young and pure and sweet he was, just to be getting his first callus.

"I have tons of calluses," Magnus said. "This is different. And it hurts."

I looked at the bump, which was near the base of Magnus's thumb and didn't in fact look like a callus at all. So this morning we went to the pediatrician, who examined Bump—by now I felt it had a separate identity—and asked Magnus how long it had been there.

"Since second grade," Magnus said.

"What grade are you in now?" asked the pediatrician.

"Fifth," Magnus said.

"I think he means fourth," I said quickly.

The pediatrician looked confused. "Do you know what grade you're in?" he asked Magnus.

"Yes, he does," I said. "What I mean is, I think the bump has been there since fourth grade, not second."

"I'm pretty sure it's been there since second grade," Magnus said, and I made a sort of helpless gesture meant to convey to the pediatrician that I'm really an excellent mother but certain things get past me.

The pediatrician thought that Magnus should get a CT, and sent us over to the radiology department of the hospital, where I had to explain to a further six layers of medical personnel that, yes, Bump appeared to be entering its fourth year of existence, but that fact in and of itself was really not an accurate reflection of my parenting skills.

Finally a technician whisked Magnus and Bump off for the CT and then Magnus and I met with the radiologist in his office. He had the CT scan of Magnus's hand up on a monitor on his desk.

"It's not a cyst or a tumor," the radiologist said. "It appears to be an embedded splinter."

Magnus looked at me.

"Oh, I'm sure it's not a splinter," I said.

"I'm sure it is," the radiologist said.

He tapped the monitor with his pencil.

"See that little object? It's obviously been embedded in his hand for several years."

Now, McSweeney's, you have to understand that Magnus is an anxious person and has several phobias. The most prominent, longstanding, fear-provoking phobia is that he'll get a splinter and that the splinter will stay stuck in his body for years—something that I have assured him many times is impossible.

"I see," I said weakly.

The radiologist went on for a little while about foreign-body granuloma and soft-tissue encapsulation and protein absorption and then I said, "But you don't know for sure it's a splinter."

The radiologist stroked his beard thoughtfully. "What else could it be?"

"A thorn," I said, feeling like a balladeer. "Maybe a thistle."

"It's not organic," the radiologist said. "I'd guess it's metal."

"A staple, then," I said. I turned to Magnus. "It's probably a staple."

"It's a splinter," the radiologist said firmly, "and at this point there's nothing we can do about it and nothing to worry about." We left shortly afterward.

In the car, I talked about irony quite a bit. I talked about the definition of irony, and how rare and interesting it was to find an event that was truly ironic. I talked about verbal irony versus situational irony, and dramatic irony. I talked about irony's rich literary history, how even Shakespeare used it, even Sophocles. I talked about irony all the way to McDonald's.

Magnus ate with one hand and stretched the other open on the tabletop so he could look at Bump. "I bet I got this at Cooley Park," he said.

"I don't know why you would think that," I said, although I had thought the same thing immediately. Cooley Park is a playground where we stopped once on a road trip and I forced my sons to play even though the playground equipment was at least forty years old and the swings hung from rusty chains twenty feet long and the seesaws were made of rotting wood bristling with splinters the size of toothpicks. It was also, inexplicably, paved with crushed gravel. The boys still have nightmares about it sometimes.

Magnus closed his hand. "You only ever take us to McDonald's when you feel bad for making us do something," he said.

I pointed a French fry at him. "That is 100 percent not true. We also come here when I'm hung over."

A woman at the table next to us was struggling to open a

ketchup packet and when I said that, she squeezed the packet so hard it flew out of her fingers and onto the floor. I gave her my good-mother look.

On the way home, Magnus was pretty quiet except for once at a stoplight, when he asked me if it was true that carpenter bees don't sting. He was clearly working his way mentally through ten years' worth of things that I'd told him and that Bump had now cast into serious doubt.

"Yes," I said, "that's true. But I may as well tell you that the car doesn't really have a backup gas tank." (One of Magnus's other phobias is the car running out of gas.)

We rode the rest of the way home in a silence as thick as a stack of towels.

Something else the radiologist told us was that the splinter would eventually work its way out, but he didn't know when. It might happen in a year, or many years, possibly even decades. The splinter may not come out of Magnus's hand until Magnus is older than I am now. Imagine that! At least I'll be free of his obviously growing skepticism by then.

And maybe by then he'll understand something: I did the best I could.

Sincerely,

KATHERINE HEINY
BETHESDA, MD

from ISSUE 51

DEAR MCSWEENEY'S,

In the course of my adult life I have voted only once, a fact I attribute to having played rugby at school.

It was not a choice. We were forced into shorts and scratchy blue jerseys. The field, in the dark of the English winter, was hard as rattan and frequently covered in frost. Adjacent to the field was an abattoir. When the wind was favorable, the smell of roasting animal flesh would drift our way in clouds.

The teacher was a baldheaded victim of testosterone poisoning who would have been at home on either side of a prison yard. His face was as red as a suckling pig's. Rumor had it he once won a drinking competition by quaffing forty-two consecutive pints of beer, leaving his opponent, a fellow teacher, naked and singing sea shanties on a bridge. He always wore a yellow tracksuit with a whistle around his neck, which he would blow and yell, "Get stuck in, lads." If you did not, he would stride over and scream heteronormative insults into your face.

The school had three teams: a first fifteen, a second, and a third. The rest of us belonged to the "rejects," which meant we played for only eighty torturous minutes every Wednesday.

I was not an aficionado of the game. There was no escape from the cold, which, with my South Indian genes, I was particularly vulnerable to. I would try to keep warm by scraping my hands against the sides of my pocketless shorts, my teeth chattering, my cheeks tear-stained. If the ball came my way I would pull my sleeves over my hands and handle it as I would an ice sculpture, presenting it to the nearest player, regardless of which side we were on. Sometimes a boy would tackle me anyway, slamming me into the ground, which felt like being struck in the flank by a stampeding boar. On occasion I would take advantage of a distracting moment in the game by making a run for it into the woods, where I would hide until the final whistle sounded. Once in a while I would forge excuse notes from my parents, claiming an ankle injury or a chest infection.

Being a nonplaying player, I did not care which position I was given so long as I did not have to step inside the "scrum," a moving, cannibalistic beast comprised of sixteen boys with interlocking heads who push, kick, bite, and butt until someone succeeds in knocking the ball backward to a member of his team. One team starts on the left, the other on the right. Both fight with all their brains, brawn, and sinews to gain ground, sometimes only inches. The aim of the game is to transport the ball to the opposite side of the field in order to win five points, which is termed a "try." At any moment, one can ascertain which side is in the ascendancy from the position of the ball, which could be near the center, or on the left, or the extreme left, or the extreme right. The ball is everything. The ball is power.

We rejects were encouraged to support the first fifteen, to wear its colors, to cheer its members. We had little choice in our affiliation: it would have been bizarre to cheer for the opposition, though I am sure there were a few renegades throughout the years who adopted such an approach. Theoretically, at least, that option was always available: rugby is not a dictatorship wherein one person sits on the ball while his teammates shoot the spectators. There are rules, a referee, governing boards, coaches, managers, experts with expert opinions. And, of course, one is free not to participate at all, to ignore the entire world of rugby, as I did, and focus on other endeavors.

But herein lies the problem. At school, rugby was the only game there was. We were told that it was good for us, that it would make us strong and fit. Many boys loved it, would speak contemptuously about those who showed little interest. To them it was *our* game, *our* team, *our* school. The school had given us rugby and it was our duty to give back to the school. The finest and most enthusiastic boys of all became team captains, decided selection and strategy, wrote match reports. Others, less skilled or athletic, played their parts by donning the school uniform on Saturdays and cheering for their classmates, rejoicing when their fellows were proved victorious. As for the rest of us, the rejects and cynics and losers and wimps, we were voiceless, faceless, and silent. Although it was true that we had chosen to reject the game, it was also true that rugby was the only game in town, a circumstance that had been decided for us, before us, in spite of us, by the school, something else none of us had chosen to go to. This, too, was something we had been born into. If we didn't go to school, we were punished and publicly shamed, forced back into line.

As I grew older, it became clear to me that the same was true of politics. In politics, the state was rugby's equivalent. There were two sides, one on the left, one on the right. Most of the players were people I would never have become friends with. They had far more in common with each other than with my peers. But every four years we were asked to declare our loyalty to one side, the ones in blue or the ones in red, and if we refused we were labeled irresponsible and ungrateful. Even if, at times, I became distracted by the spectacle of the game, when the final whistle sounded I was always left with the same singular truth: I had not chosen this game. It had been imposed on me. And whether I voted or not, this would always be the case.

Some years ago I learned of another game played for centuries in the Amazonian jungle. As in rugby, there are two teams. Each forms a line and lifts a heavy tree trunk onto their shoulders. Thus burdened, the two teams run toward the finish line, moving as fast as they can. If one team is struggling, however, a member of the opposing side crosses over and assists them. The aim is for both teams to finish at the same time.

Had I been born into a society that played this game, I suspect I would have had more interest in politics. I would have joined in gladly, even enthusiastically. I would have participated; I would have cheered; I would have played. But this is not the way it works. We do not get to choose the games we play. We can opt in or we can opt out, but the game is fixed.

Sincerely,

RAJEEV BALASUBRAMANYAM
BERLIN, GERMANY

from ISSUE 34

DEAR MCSWEENEY'S,

You know when you're at an awkward Q&A after a reading or something, and somebody stands up and says, "I have more of a comment than a question"? Because I love that.

JULIE KLAUSNER
NEW YORK, NY

DEAR EDITOR,

Did you know that Jerry Lewis turned down the role of the killer in *Cruising*, the lead in *Being There*, and the title role in *Charly*? What's more, he turned down the Robert Shaw part in *Jaws*, and the role of Salieri in *Amadeus*. Also, Peter Ustinov's part in *Logan's Run*. Can you imagine him as Humbert Humbert? Apparently he couldn't. And we will never have the privilege of knowing how he would have handled *Portnoy's Complaint*—he turned down a chance to star in and direct that film. He was also screen-tested for the Sterling Hayden role in *The Godfather* and the John Hurt role in *Alien*, though it was unclear if he was actually offered these parts or not. How different might be the history of American film in the '70s had he actually taken the roles of the wire-tapper in *The Conversation*, Popeye Doyle in *The French Connection*, or Lex Luthor in *Superman*—though I suppose we can be grateful to him, in a sense, for the opportunities given Gene Hackman, who certainly did not disappoint in these parts. Nor is it likely he could have improved on Jason Robards's portrayal of Ben Bradlee in *All the President's Men,* or on Rip Torn's performance in *The Man Who Fell to Earth*. Perhaps most frustrating for the film buff is the knowledge that Alfred Hitchcock, the Master of Suspense, died before casting Lewis in a thriller. Lewis had previously turned down the Martin Balsam part in *Psycho* and the Sean Connery part in *Marnie*. Equally tantalizing is the large Lewis role trimmed out of *Nashville* during last-minute edits—in interviews Lewis claims it as his masterwork. Robert Altman attempted to make it up for him, but an embittered Lewis turned down parts in Altman's next seven films. He also turned down the parts that went to Walter Matthau in both *Charley Varrick* and *King Creole,* thus missing his chance to work with veteran director Don Siegel (as well as to appear opposite Elvis Presley). He also turned down the John Lithgow part in *Blow Out* and the part that was reworked for Richard Pryor in *Blue Collar*. He refused the part Jack Lemmon played in *The China Syndrome,* though it was later pointed out that the role was developed for Lemmon and Lewis was never offered it. He also refused the role of the off-screen voice of Charlie in the hit television series *Charlie's Angels*, a role later taken by John Forsyth, later of *Dynasty*. Unquestionably, *Excalibur* would have been a different film completely had Lewis not dropped out during the first week of shooting to be replaced by Nicol Williamson as Merlin. He also turned down the role of the arsonist in *Body Heat*.

Strangely, Jerry Lewis was never considered for any part by Michael Cimino.

JONATHAN LETHEM
BROOKLYN, NY

DEAR MCSWEENEY'S,

The animal trials held in Burgundy in the sixteenth and seventeenth centuries can provide a striking and potentially instructive parallel to the military infrastructure of war-worn Iraq.

In 1522, for example, the barley crops surrounding a certain village were destroyed by rats. The villagers immediately hired a prosecutor who charged the rats with "wanton destruction" and brought the case before a special church-run court. The vicar who presided over that court appointed a lawyer to represent the rats, set a date for trial, and read the summons (addressed to "some rats of the diocese") from the steps of the church.

When the trial date rolled around, "some rats" failed to appear in court. Bartholomew Chassenee, the rats' lawyer, argued that the rats must not have heard the summons. Moreover, the summons only addressed "some" of the rats within the church's jurisdiction. Even if a rat had happened to hear the summons, how could he know whether or not he himself was expected to appear?

The court accepted this argument and ordered a second summons, addressing "all" the rats of the diocese, to be read from the pulpit of every local parish church.

The rats failed to appear a second time. Chassenee argued that the defendants were widely dispersed and needed more time to make preparations for the journey. The court accepted this argument as well and granted a further delay in the proceedings.

When the rats failed to appear a third time, Chassenee was ready with a third argument. It was well established at the time that if a person was summoned to appear in court but could not do so safely (for example, because of the pestilence) he could lawfully refuse to obey the writ of summons. Chassenee argued that the rats were likely to be attacked by cats if they attempted to make the journey to court, and so they should not be required to make the trip. The court debated whether or not to issue an order enjoining the villagers to restrain their cats. Unable to arrive at a conclusion, they adjourned the question, and judgment for the rats was eventually granted by default.

Chassenee went on to become a successful judge and sometimes cited cases involving animals and insects in his decisions regarding human beings. For example, when he was heading a panel of judges considering an appeal from a death sentence made by a group of convicted heretics, he agreed to give them a hearing because they were no lower than rats, and even rats have a right to be heard. Unfortunately for the defendants, Chassenee died on the eve of the hearing, and all the heretics were promptly exterminated.

The implications are obvious and troubling.

Allegedly,

ANNA PERVUKHIN
STUDENT OF LAW
CHICAGO, IL

DEAR MCSWEENEY'S,
I wish to call my letter:

NATIONALISM ROUNDUP.

Here it goes, in four episodes.

1. A friend of mine once gave a speech about Bosnia to an international relations department at a famous Midwestern university. I attended his speech. After he finished, a group of hangers-on, all men except for me, stuck around to debate the finer points of the former Yugoslavia. The conversation was very detailed, including references to specific mayors of specific Croatian villages. It was like record collector geek talk, only about Bosnia. They were the record collectors of Bosnia. So they went on denouncing the various idiotic nationalist causes of various splinter groups, blaming nationalism itself for the genocide war. And of course a racist nationalism is to blame. But the more they ranted, the more uncomfortable I became. They, many of them

immigrants themselves, considered patriotic allegiance to be a sin, a divisive, villainous drive leading to exclusion, hate, and murder. I, heretofore silent, spoke up. This is what I said. I said that I had recently flown over Memphis, Tennessee. I said that the idea of Memphis, Tennessee, not to mention looking down at it, made me go all soft. Because I looked down at Memphis, Tennessee and thought of all my heroes who had walked its streets. I thought of Sun Records, of producer Sam Phillips. Sam Phillips, who once described the sort of person he recorded as "a person who had dreamed, and dreamed, and dreamed." A person like Elvis Presley, his funny bass player Bill Black, his guitarist Scottie Moore (we have the same birthday, he and I). Jerry Lee Lewis. Carl Perkins. Howlin' Wolf. *Hello, I'm Johnny Cash*. I told the Bosnian record collectors that when I thought of the records of these Memphis men, when I looked out the window at the Mississippi mud and felt their names moistening my tongue, that what I felt, what I was proud to feel, was patriotic. Then one man, from some –bekistan I'd never heard of, looked me in the eye and delivered the following warning. "Those," he said, "are the seeds of war."

2. You know what word I never use? *Absolutely*. I cannot bring myself to say this word. Every time someone else does, a picture flashes in my head. When someone answers a question about whether she liked a certain movie or if he's voting for so-and-so or whatever, the picture that flashes in my head is the illustration of Napoleon crowning himself emperor from my tenth-grade world history textbook. When someone says, "Absolutely. You couldn't be more right," I am distracted by the image of a little man putting a golden hat on his little head. *Absolutely* seems kind of

un-American. As if someone answered a waiter's query about fresh pepper on a salad with "Despotically, I'd love some." Like, "Fresh pepper?" "Yes, autocratically!" I prefer the word *sure*. No French dictators come to mind with *sure*. *Yep* is also nice, having a kind of Gary-Cooper-saving-the-town-by-his-lonesome sort of air.

3. Speaking of words. The other day I took a boat tour up the Hudson to see the home of Washington Irving. And after we traipsed through his rooms—and saw the portrait of his one true love (who died of "galloping consumption" before they were wed) and so he never married, and carried her picture everywhere—we got back on the bus and went to Sleepy Hollow to see a seventeenth-century Dutch farm. At the farm, there was a different tour guide at each station—the bridge, the mill, the manor, the tenant farmer's cabin—and to a man (they were all women, actually) they described the farm's slaves not as slaves but as "enslaved Africans." As in, the mill was worked by enslaved Africans. Or, that was the job of the enslaved Africans. After a while I couldn't stand it anymore and cornered one of these shawl-wearing tour guides and asked point blank why on earth nobody used the word *slave*. She said, "Because 'enslaved African' describes slavery as something that was done to them instead of what they were. Enslavement was not their whole identity." Um, isn't the whole dastardly point about being a slave that you don't have a choice to be anything else? That adjective, meant to pretty up an evil noun, makes "enslaved African" sound nonchalant. As in, those were the cabins of jolly Leprechauns. Or, the handsome teenagers ground the corn. Adjective, verb. The raspberry jam enjoyed by her first cousin in his fine home was lovingly prepared by an

enslaved African. Here's a good word: *slave*. *Slave*'s a good word because it is strong and ugly and therefore perfect to describe the thing it describes.

4. Not to get all we-the-people, but the other day I watched a woman walk in front of an ambulance. I mean, there are so few outlets, really, for an idealistic lazy person to do any good in the world, right? Most people seem to light up when they hear a siren, clearing to the sidewalks, cars pulling over en masse, that bubbly feeling you're part of things, a good citizen, a kind and wise old soul. But this woman, this traitor, stepped right in front of her probably dying fellow American and made the ambulance screech brakes so she could cross the street a second and a half faster than everybody else. My only hope is that one day an ambulance runs her over and an ambulance has to be called and on the way to the hospital in her ambulance someone just like her keeps getting in its way and she dies right there in the white van with the cursing medic.

SARAH VOWELL
NEW YORK, NY

DEAR MCSWEENEY'S,

I've been looking for material that your readers might find interesting, and I think I have something. Following are the world's worst cities to visit if they are named after local landmarks:

> Liverpool (England)
> Braintree (Massachusetts)
> Peabody (Massachusetts)
> Medicine Hat (Alberta)
> Worms (Germany)
> Urine (Illinois)
> Colostomy (Tunisia)
> Scrotum (Connecticut)
> King of Prussia (Pennsylvania)
> Smyrna (Georgia)

All the best,

DON STEINBERG
CENTRAL PENNSYLVANIA

DEAR DON,

Thank you. Are these real? I grew up in Illinois, though never heard of Urine.

EDITOR

DEAR EDITOR,

They start out real, but there weren't enough real ones to be funny, so 6, 7, and 8 are fake. So for true students of humor it almost has an evolving narrative in there. Also, I think Smyrna is actually in Tennessee and Medicine Hat is in Arizona.

DON

DEAR DON,

You know what might be funny: list them as it is, but somewhere indicate that we made some of them up. Then say something like: "They start out real, but there weren't enough real ones to be funny, so 6, 7, and 8 are fake."

EDITOR

DEAR EDITOR,

Sounds good to me. Also, Medicine Hat is actually in Alberta, Canada, as originally indicated.

DON

DEAR MCSWEENEY'S,

I love four-way stops. I love magnanimously directing another car to go through if the right of way isn't obvious. We all look like kings doing that little wave. At the four-way stop, we take a moment to achieve clarity, consensus, to co-sign a little group reality.

Yes, you did get here first. I see you!

Ugh, you go. I'm making a left.

Thanks, but you go. I'm about to do something real weird because I actually need to park back there. [Strange swirly motion with index finger pointed at ceiling of car and embarrassed shrug.]

Whenever I think about four-way stops, I also start thinking about health care and whether or not it's a human right. People are always so performatively skeptical about that, like: *Gee, I don't know,* is *it a human right?* Like there's a microscope they can go look in to see if there are human rights cells present in the health care.

I want to say to them out of the side of my mouth: *Don't you know? We made that shit up! The right to the pursuit of happiness— that's not real! There is no right to anything, but, like, especially not that one—are you five? You're a hairless ape. We took over the planet. Any of this ringing a bell? You don't even really have a name, if we're getting right down to it. We're all just pretending you do; that's what a name is.*

Human rights are like the four-way stop. We made it up, and we all pretend it exists because life is just better that way. But you don't *have* to let the car to your right go first. Civility isn't some kind of natural law. You could just smash into that bitch. Fuck her. You don't *have* to build a just society. Why should you pay for some stranger's chemo?

My youngest son says "butt crack" all the time. He is four. Sometimes he chants it over and over, especially when he is excited because we are going somewhere he wants to go, for instance Round Table Pizza: "Butt crack, butt crack, butt craaaaack!" he says as he bounces in his booster seat. Sometimes he uses it as an answer to a question. "Have you brushed your teeth?" "Butt CRACK!" To fully understand the effect, you have to know that he is chubby and blond with a pronounced underbite and chipped front teeth that make him look like a little bulldog.

For a while, it was only "butt crack," but now "penis" and "vagina" have joined the fray. He uses them as verbs. Once, to his brother: "Stop that or I'll penis ya iPad!"

"Are you threatening to rub your penis on your brother's iPad?" I asked.

"No!" he said, scandalized. "I was just tryna say I was gonna break it!"

The other day, I asked him if he liked hummus, and he said, "I don't vagina that," and he explained that the word *vagina* also means "love."

He is able to contain himself at school and for the most part he keeps it together in public as well, except for once at the supermarket when I was ignoring him in the checkout line because I was interacting with the credit card machine, and he said, "Mmm... vagina," and rubbed his belly. He had caught sight of the Wheat Thins. He loves Wheat Thins.

What should I do, McSweeney's? Is my little bulldog pup destined to grow up a pervert? I tried asking him to merely replace the talismanic words with stand-ins, and he picked *coconut* for *vagina*, a good choice, I thought. And for *penis* he chose *Donald Trump*. He has already intuited that the word *Trump* is hyper-charged for adults, much like other potty words. "I'm gonna Trump you up," he threatens his brother.

"Your Donald Trump is looking awfully big today, Mommy!" I do not have a penis, but it did get a laugh out of me.

Because, you see, my son does know that he is just a hairless ape, bouncing up and down, excited to go to Round Table Pizza. Words are made up; we decide what they mean. Look, he just made *coconut* mean "vagina" and *vagina* mean "love"!

BUTT CRAAAAACCKKK!!!!

Maybe I could bring myself to discipline him if it didn't delight and please me so much. Because Mommy loves all those fake, made-up things: words, human rights, four-way stops. Bounce, little chimp: let us make a better world together! Universal pre-K, preventive care, coconut, Donald Trump, BUUUUTTTT CRAAACCKKK!

Really, we get to be alive for only a little while. My son won't say "butt crack" forever, and I am going to miss it so much when he stops. He'll start believing in all sorts of made-up things without understanding that they're made-up. He will believe certain shoes are cool and other shoes are not cool. He will write a school essay agonizing over the Second Amendment and what the founders of our country intended. He will learn about the ego and the id, and tell me about them as though they are real things. And I will have to watch him forget everything he once knew so effortlessly.

The truth is, the good made-up things (novels, human rights, the tango) and the bad made-up things (designer clothes, white supremacy, corporations) have one important thing in common: they are made up. And you know what that means. We're in charge. [*Finger guns*] We're steering the ship. We can sail toward Round Table Pizza; we can stop building detention camps at the border and putting little kids in them. We make of this world what we want. And maybe that's the scariest part. We could be doing anything, and instead we're doing this.

No, you go. I'm about to do a weird thing because I actually need to park back there.

With much vagina,

RUFI THORPE
LOS ANGELES, CA

DEAR MCSWEENEY'S,

I read with amusement the exchange about towns with names like "scrotum." It seems, however, that your readers have overlooked several other places in America with names which sound a bit like body parts. There is, for example, a Urethra, Michigan. Don't forget Melanoma Valley, California; Beloit College's Hippo Campus; and Surgical Scar, New Mexico.

GAVIN BRUCE
FORMERLY OF TOPEKA

from ISSUE 48

DEAR MCSWEENEY'S,

I'm worried about our cat. He is extremely vocal, pretty much all of the time. He meows in the morning, when it's time to get up. He meows at seemingly random intervals throughout the night. He meows when I get home and put my keys in the dish in the hallway. Food, affection, playtime—these things distract him, but not for long.

We took him to the vet and she said there was nothing wrong with him. She suggested we get a device that pumps a calming pheromone into the house at all times. It is called Feliway.

Feliway.

She also said that he has a "youthful voice." That is because, when he meows, he sounds like an infant screaming.

My wife and I have been married for just over a year. The cat was our inheritance from an unrelated tragedy. Since acquiring it, we've purchased a cat tower. We've purchased Da Bird, a popular cat toy composed of a plastic rod and several feathers, with which one can tease the cat. We bought a woven wool basket, just barely the size of our cat if he were to curl into a ball and stay put, called a Cat Cave. He's never made it inside—he has no interest in climbing in, regardless of the treats we hide in there—so now we put our appliance cables in it, to keep them coiled and off the floor.

It's entirely possible that the cat is damaged. He has been through a lot. It is also entirely possible that he's after one small, simple thing, and we just can't figure it out.

He loves us. He is extremely affectionate. In fact, earlier tonight I speculated that perhaps he's meowing to make sure that we're ready for whatever it is he's about to do next. I was a little bit like this as a child.

The vet said the pheromone the device releases is the same as what the cat releases when he rubs his cheeks against our knuckles, the chair legs, the edges of my laptop, etc.—which he is always doing. The device plugs into the wall and pumps that pheromone into the house. We're supposed to put it near where he spends most of his time, but it's hard to know where that is when we're not around, because when we're around he just wants to sit on our chests and rub his cheek against us.

We feed him well, but he is still very thin.

The vet said, "Most cats are fat. He's just one of those cats that knows how much to eat."

We feed him bits of chicken from dinner sometimes, but that only makes him howl and meow more, when there's no chicken to offer.

I read a blog post that said we're not supposed to engage with him when he meows. Any response reinforces the idea that meowing will get him what he wants. And he probably doesn't know that we don't actually know what he wants.

When we brought him home from the vet, he tore his claws out, anxiously working the small holes in the walls of the carrier. He bled in the carrier, tracked blood into the house. He howled.

Most nights, he sleeps between us like a toddler. He gets

under the comforter, settles it at his neck. Last night, he set his cheek against the corner of my pillow.

I should take a moment to reestablish that we are good cat owners. Or relatively good. We make a point of trying, and we care. We also have a wonderful network of supportive friends who help care for the cat while we're away for various social or professional obligations. We provide the majority of things one might think a cat would want.

And yet, he meows.

It's rarely directed at us, directly. Typically, he perches on the corner of the bed and meows out into the room. Away from us. Out into the hollows. Or he'll sit in the corner of the kitchen and meow into the hallway. He looks away from us. He stares off at what seems like nothing. He meows and meows and meows.

I put fresh food in the bowl. Clean the water dish and refill it. I whip Da Bird around like a tassel. I drag it across the comforter.

If you have any thoughts on any of this, I would truly love to hear them.

Sincerely,

COLIN WINNETTE
SAN FRANCISCO, CA

from ISSUE 39

DEAR McSWEENEY'S,

Here's what I want to know: when you don't realize that a crime
you committed was a "real" type of crime, and so you fail to tell
a prospective employer about it, is that tantamount to covering it
up? I didn't think so, but this human-resources company seems
to. When I told their guy, Reed, that "maybe it was a 'you had
to be there' kind of thing, but I bet you wouldn't have realized
it was a misdemeanor, either," the voice at the other end of the
line was far from sympathetic, and not nearly as musical as the
name I've made up for him might suggest.

Trespassing, I have come to understand, is something that
will show up on a background check. Legally, I am not at liberty
to say where I applied for this job, but I'll divulge that the
company is involved in "searching" the "internet." Given that
the place was founded on background-checking everything in
the entire world, it was probably a little foolish of me not to
make a mental sweep of the dusty corners of my life before I sat
down for the interview.

And of course, the I-9 application I filled out a few days later
wasn't *designed* to help me remember my criminal record, but

wouldn't it have been nice if it had been? "Have you ever been convicted of a misdemeanor or felony? Caught red-handed in an unlucky moment of public urination? No judgments here; we've all done it from time to time. Or maybe you and your friends were looking for a secret swimming hole five years ago, and the only path just so happened to cut through some property owned by the Girl Scouts? Think really hard before checking YES or NO. *Think*, Marco..."

An impractical vision, sure. But consider, to use the internet developers' term, the basic *usability* of those employment forms. Reed said I had to complete them on a PC, and since my parents live too far away for me to use theirs, I went to my public library. Once there, so many pop-up windows interrupted my experience that I might as well have been filling the thing out while driving and texting. After each page loaded, I received a warning: *This page contains both secure and nonsecure items. Do you want to display the nonsecure items?* The first fifteen times, I selected NO. Then I thought, What if the nonsecure items are really important? So I clicked YES the next thirty-five times. Unlike with the law, there seemed to be no right answer.

More boxes demanded my attention, pop-ups within pop-ups. As I finished each page, I was asked to electronically sign it. This brought up another box: *To the best of your knowledge, is the information contained herein true and correct?* Once, with this box, I accidentally clicked NO, confusing it with the nonsecure-items box. Luckily, the startled grunt I let out didn't disturb any of the library's other patrons, and I was able to change my answer.

But can I really blame my carelessness on pop-up windows alone? A good deal of culpability rests on the soft shoulders of a woman whom I'll call Trixie. Trixie with her long legs, interestingly dyed hair, and mild acne. Unlike Reed, her fake name is telling. She was our travel agent to this secret brook, talking up its amenities, describing imaginary photos from an unprinted brochure. On our hike to the spot, we passed two girls hightailing it back down to the banks of a sunny river wherein scores of law-abiding citizens floated, contented people who didn't want any more secrets in their lives. "Mum's the word," one of the retreating girls said, "but I wouldn't go up there."

Trixie pressed her for more information, but we all knew what was waiting ahead. For a moment, we stood at that spot—what I now think of as my "line of liability"—and somehow Trixie convinced everyone that the girls were lying. They were trying to protect the swimming location, using an antiquated British idiom to throw us off. Though she'd forgotten their names, Trixie admitted that she'd had an altercation with one of them in the past. The police couldn't *possibly* be hiding out up there, she insisted, only sixty feet around the bend.

Seems to me that the dumbest sins are the ones you have to atone for again and again. Lesson learned.

Yours,

MARCO KAYE
HOBOKEN, NJ

DEAR MCSWEENEY'S,

I predict that there will come a day when you are, let's say, forty-nine. You will visit your personal archive that you've placed in a box on the top shelf of a closet at your mother's house. By then you will be either incredibly successful and will want to look back fondly at your humble beginnings, or you will have plummeted into total obscurity and confusion and you will want to look back at your glory days when you actually had something going. Or perhaps you will just want to give yourself a little private retrospective, as you near your half-century mark. In any case, at that time, which seems so far away now but is really just around the corner, you will tenderly unwrap that great Issue No. 3 of *McSweeney's* etc. etc. from its archival tissue paper. No matter how far or how close you hold it from your face and no matter which of your glasses you are wearing—your distance glasses, your reading glasses, your graduated trifocals—you will not be able to read a fucking word of that tiny, tiny, tiny, tiny, tiny, tiny type.

    Love,

PETRA EHRENZWEIG

DEAR MCSWEENEY'S,

I wrote you yesterday asking about an interview with Helen Hunt that you may or may not have published. While doing laundry this morning, I remembered that she was wearing a tealish sweater on the cover, either yours or *Redbook*'s. Thought that might help.

Thanks again,

JEN STATSKY
NEW YORK, NY

from ISSUE 37

HEY MCSWEENEY'S,

While making my latest crossword, I had to stop for a good couple of minutes to contemplate two answers I'd managed to fit in the southwest corner: VIMEO (clued as "YouTube competitor") and AMANPOUR ("News anchor Christiane").

Both fit; that's always a plus.

Both were new, never-before-used entries, and us puzzle makers love being the first to debut new words in crosswords.

But the fact that VIMEO crossed AMANPOUR at the M really bothered me. Was that unfair? Just how well-known are those entries? Would most people have heard of both words?

I think about things like this all day. Crossword constructors are supposed to go out of their way to avoid obscure crossings. When we have to rely upon an ungainly entry, like the Belgian river MEUSE, to hold our answer grids together, we'd better be damned sure that the words going the other way are all common entries. If we crossed the first E in MEUSE with something like SOTER (you recall the years of this papacy, 166–175 AD, no doubt), we'd be stuck with a blind crossing. *Blind* because that crossing square is essentially unsolvable without either an encyclopedic knowledge of arcana or mad Googling skills.

In certain circles, these blind crossings are called Naticks. I should know, because one of my puzzles led to the coining of that term. In my Sunday *New York Times* crossword of July 6, 2008, two obscure entries crossed 1-Across, of all places. *"Treasure Island* illustrator, 1911" clued N C WYETH, while "Town at the eighth mile of the Boston Marathon" clued (you guessed it) NATICK.

The N was completely blind.

I remember thinking at the time that it was a tough but essentially fair crossing. Then again, I live in Boston and have at least thought about running the Boston Marathon. So NATICK to me would have been a no-brainer. Not so to pretty much everybody else. Since WYETH's name began with two initials, that first letter could have been anything. Which meant the Boston town could have been BATICK or HATICK or MATICK. You get the idea.

This move was deemed extremely dickish, and the Natick principle was formed: "If you include a proper noun that you cannot reasonably expect more than one-quarter of the solving public to have heard of, you must cross that noun with a reasonably common word or phrase."

So what do you think? Is VIMEO crossing AMANPOUR a Natick? Let me know.

BRENDAN EMMETT QUIGLEY
CAMBRIDGE, MA

DEAR MCSWEENEY'S,

Here are some phrases I intend to work into conversation whenever possible:

1. The ground cannot cause a fumble.
2. Right ho!
3. There will be a reckoning.

Sincerely,

KIERSTEN CONNER-SAX

DEAR MCSWEENEY'S,

Let's Kill Carlo is a game we used to play at the dinner table when I was young. We'd be there making fun of each other and drinking, the adults with their wine, us kids with our *agua fresca*—there was a strict no-alcohol policy for anyone under twelve—when someone would say, "There was an earthquake in Oaxaca last week." Or, "Did you hear about the plane crash in Colombia?" Or, "Apparently some reactor exploded in Russia." Immediately, the rest of us would chime in, "Let's kill Carlo!" That's how the game would start. Now, Carlo, in case you were wondering, was my brother.

Let's back up a bit here.

In 1973, my mom—I'll call her Maria, since that's actually her name—graduated from high school in Mexico City and enrolled in college. She had three months of vacation before her and also some savings, so she signed up for an Italian summer course in Perugia. One day, while she was there, she walked into a grocery store and instantly fell in love with the man handling the fruit. A few weeks later, she had moved in with the *fruttivendolo*, Elio, who happened to be a medical student.

She would end up spending half a decade in Italy.

Maria also decided to go ahead with the degree she had intended to pursue back in Mexico. She'd study by herself all semester long, and then fly home to take her exams and see her family. Every time she went home, her grandmother would make the same scene. It played out like a *telenovela*:

> ABUELA: Stop living in sin! I'll pay for the wedding!

> MARIA: I already told you, Elio can't leave the country!

> ABUELA: Why is that again?

> MARIA: Because military service is mandatory for all men in Italy. Unless you're studying medicine; then you're exempt, but they won't give you a passport.

> ABUELA: Right... But can't we have the wedding anyway? At my house?

And that, *McSweeney's*, is exactly what they did. Maria and Elio got married at Grandma's house by proxy. My mom's uncle stood in for the groom, holding a letter of attorney signed by Elio, who celebrated all by himself back in Perugia. Years later, a picture of that wedding still hung on our wall. It didn't bother my father or me—after all, it's just my mom in a pretty dress, holding a bunch of flowers.

The trouble was that medical students were only exempt from military service while they were students. Upon graduation they were still expected to put in a year, usually stationed far from home. Unless you were a *capofamiglia*, "a head of the family." When Elio's last semester rolled around, he and Maria started panicking. A year apart was out of the question. But so was having a baby. They couldn't even afford new winter coats, and whatever extra money they made went toward airfare to Mexico. Elio was in his finals when Maria had to leave for yet another round of her own exams.

Now, you may not know this, McSweeney's, but because we Mexicans are not really used to laws being enforced, we tend to view them as negotiable. This begins to explain why, upon returning to Mexico, Maria asked to borrow a baby. It was Carlos, the newborn boy of the *señora* who took care of her grandma. "Take him to the park," said the *señora*, assuming that my mother wanted to get some practice caring for a newborn. But of course, Maria never made it to the park. Instead, she pushed the stroller right over to the *registro civil*. Too nervous to come up with a name, she just Italianized "Carlos" and attached her husband's surname to the end of it. And that's how, without ever being born, my half-brother, Carlo Moretti, came into existence.

By dinnertime, the baby was home and Maria was on a plane to Perugia—a mother in name only. The fake birth certificate worked like a charm, and Elio got a permanent exemption from service. Carlos with an *s* never knew about this ingenious, utterly illegal exploitation of his weeks-old self, and neither did his mom. In fact, after Elio and Maria split up five years later and Maria moved back to Mexico, no one gave Carlo Moretti another thought. At least not until the day Elio phoned our place. He and Maria had kept in touch; to me, he was like a distant uncle who calls on birthdays. But this time he had shocking news: Carlo had come of age, and now he was being called up for military service.

That morning eighteen years earlier, Maria had been worried only about her immediate future. It never crossed her mind that she could—that indeed she *should*—have made Carlo a Carla. But now it was too late, and the army was inquiring about Carlo's whereabouts. First letters, then calls, then visits. All Elio could say was that he had no idea. But they weren't buying it; people have been known to try all sorts of things to avoid service, and having your father lie for you was about as common as saying you had flat feet. Elio then tried arguing that, for all he knew, Carlo might be dead. "In that case," they said, "where's the death certificate?"

It was in a collaborative effort to answer this very question, McSweeney's, that we played Let's Kill Carlo for the first time. Rather seriously. We were brainstorming plausible deaths so that Elio, without having to produce a cadaver, could have a solid story to tell the soldiers at his door. I was seven years old, and I proposed a scuba-diving accident—body never found. People clapped. I was awfully good at Let's Kill Carlo. And it really was a special game. It felt purposeful and inclusive. Visitors, it turned out, were always eager to point out the potential ways a person could disappear off the face of the Earth. I remember how one time my cousin's new girlfriend suggested spontaneous combustion. This idea was quickly dismissed, but we were smitten with her. Let's Kill Carlo became something of a litmus test: if a guest was too proper to play, we knew they'd never be one of us.

When I was nine, my mom and I went to Italy. It was my first trip to Europe, and alongside postcard memories of tiny Fiats, gelato, and couples petrified mid-embrace in volcanic ash, one image stands out. We're in a bleak office. My feet dangle from a chair while Maria and Elio explain the Carlo predicament to two lawyers. The *avvocati* leap out of their chairs, deploying an impressive range of gestures. *"Porca madonna! Il santo esercito!"* they yell.

I don't remember what followed this choreography of disapproval, but I know that after a couple of years of paperwork, the *avvocati* managed to conjure up what Elio needed: a death certificate. That's why we haven't played Let's Kill Carlo lately—there's no use for it anymore. Anyway, I'm not sure we could enjoy it these days. It would be all too easy to come up with possibilities in Mexico, where tens of thousands have disappeared in the past few years. It would be too macabre even for us, especially considering that the families of the disappeared often receive nothing from the authorities: no investigation, and definitely not a death certificate.

LAIA JUFRESA
MADRID, SPAIN

from ISSUE 50

DEAR MCSWEENEY'S,

I was in Japan earlier this year for a project and had the chance to meander around a little. I had mentioned to my friend Risa that I was interested in seeing sumo. I wanted to draw the wrestlers if I could. She said it wasn't really the season but maybe we could see them training somewhere. She called around and I think it was a bit of a stretch but one of the trainers at one of the places said we could come there one morning to see them working out.

I got to the train stop where we were meeting early so I went to a convenience store called Family Mart. I got this really good melon bread (that I want again right now).

We met on the corner and walked over. The place was little and nothing special from the outside but really impressive inside. We took off our shoes and there were four pillows on the ground for us to sit on (there were two strangers there doing the same thing we were doing). About eight large guys were on the dirt floor that was a step down from where we were sitting. They were taking turns wrestling each other or doing exercises or drinking water or sweeping the dirt. There was one guy that was a little smaller (maybe he was younger?) and he was really being pushed physically by the other wrestlers. He was making this really intense guttural noise and at one point I moved my sketchpad from my lap to behind me because I thought he was going to puke on us.

The coach yelled out loud orders. (I didn't know what he was saying; he just sounded like any coach.) He was sitting next to us. I was beginning to get a little uncomfortable on the floor (because I am so out of shape—this seemed like a metaphor for something at the time, getting uncomfortable while watching

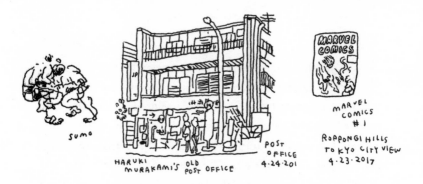

SUMO

HARUKI MURAKAMI'S OLD POST OFFICE

POST OFFICE 4·24·201

MARVEL COMICS # 1

ROPPONGI HILLS TOKYO CITY VIEW 4·23·2017

strangely strong men exerting this amount of energy) so I rear-ranged a little. After a couple minutes, my feet started to fall asleep so I turned a little again. I was kind of embarrassed because there were only four of us and I was the only one squirming all over every couple of minutes. I could hold a position for a bit and then I would need to rearrange my legs.

The coach continued to yell at the wrestlers as they took turns plowing into each other. It sounded like a strong clap when they would embrace in the middle. I drew several pictures that all mostly ended up looking the same because they were all large men pushing against each other.

An even bigger clothed wrestler man walked in. Risa nudged me to make sure I realized he was there. I got the idea that the enormous guys we were watching were younger wrestlers that were training and were not even as enormous as the older, more experienced professionals. After a couple more minutes I rearranged again.

Just then the coach stood up, walked behind a sliding door, grabbed a little folding chair, and handed it to me. It was about 130 percent embarrassing but I thanked him a lot, unfolded

NEWSSTAND IN FRONT OF SHIBUYA MARK CITY 4·28·2017

DUCK IN YOYOGI PARK 4·24·2017

THERE IS A MAN HOLDING A HAWK.

HEDGEHOG IN HARRY HEDGEHOG CAFE HARAJUKU 4·24·2017

~$86 MANGO AT KYOBASHI SEMBIKIYA

it, and sat on it. I couldn't figure out if it was because I was driving him crazy, or if he actually just wanted me to feel better (I assume about fifty-fifty).

We left a few minutes later after thanking the coach and another trainer (that I think may have been the one Risa talked to on the phone). It felt weird to be outside. We could hear them through the window as we tied our shoes. We then got coffee and went to a park.

JASON POLAN
NEW YORK, NY

from ISSUE 8

DEAR KEVIN,

That business about "the benign manipulation of luring people" makes me think you work in advertising. In advertising circles is there a word for what you're proposing? Is there something that advertising folks know that fiction-writing folks either don't know or don't, for whatever reason, spend much time thinking about?

EDITOR

DEAR EDITOR,

In advertising, the word for the "benign manipulation" of people
is "advertising." But that's an interesting question. I think lots
of people suspect that advertising creatives have all sorts of
secret knowledge about psychology and mind control, which we
routinely use to manipulate consumers to act against their own
free will, as if Foote Cone Belding recruits its art directors from
the School of the Americas. Maybe folks believe this because
so much of television advertising is rooted in misdirection.
The next time you're watching a program, count how many
commercials at first pretend to be an ad for something else.
I've done it in spots, too, and I wonder why that is. I think
it's because the inversion of the viewer's expectations forces
some into a response, good or bad, and the only reaction every
advertiser fears, of course, is indifference. I suppose the same is
true for writers. That's why I want to put the e-mail addresses
at the bottom of the story. It's a call to action, just as the person
is feeling relief or anger or surprise. Let it out! Write to me!

KEVIN GUILFOILE
CHICAGO, IL

DEAR MCSWEENEY'S,

I've decided to come clean about some of my perfect capers. The perfect capers started the summer between second and third grades, when I decided I wanted people to think the school bathroom was haunted. My first idea was that I would leave letters written by pirates under the benches, or behind the sink. My aunt and I worked out a system for aging paper (we'd burn it over the gas stove) and I practiced writing with a brush pen. Sometimes the paper would light up in our hands, or get burnt black. Eventually, I got it right: a perfect piece that read, "Ye are in my bathroom."

I left the letter behind the sink, and no one found it for a while. Then, when they found it, they all knew it was fake. Anybody else would've thrown in the towel, but after all that work with aging the paper, I had a fire in me. I bought a rubber hand from the toy store. I came into the bathroom a little bit before the other girls were due to change for swimming and I stuck the rubber hand into an AC vent in the ceiling. When the girls saw the hand, they ran out of the bathroom all at once. Then, I climbed up onto the changing stall wall, where I could perch, and I tucked the hand back into the AC vent.

I did this a couple of times that summer. After a while, the teachers wouldn't even listen when the girls tried to tell them about the hand.

"There's no hand in the bathroom," the principal said.

At around this time, my mom was working at Herman Hospital, where there was about a three-foot crawlspace between the ceiling and the floor. If you wanted to, you could move an insulation tile aside and crawl around in that space. There were rumors that people were living there. No one believed the rumors, at least my mom didn't, until she came into the break room one night and saw a naked old man with a long beard leap monkey-like onto the counter, onto the refrigerator, and then up into the ceiling. He left a pile of half-eaten doughnuts on the floor. He'd been eating them Indian-style.

Then there was the time at summer camp. I was nine, at a camp where the minimum age was eleven. There was me and one other nine-year-old girl, named Susan, and all the other kids were eleven, twelve, thirteen, fourteen, and fifteen. There was this kid Chuck who was fourteen who used to beat me and Susan up. One night, he threw Susan against a wall. So Susan and I saved our urine for a week. We saved it in a gigantic plastic packaging bag we found inside a gigantic cardboard box. For a solid week, we both peed into the big bag. Then we poured the pee all over Chuck's bed. No one caught us, and no one suspected us.

More soon. I still have to tell you about the greatest of all capers.

Sincerely,

AMIE BARRODALE
BROOKLYN, NY

DEAR MCSWEENEY'S,

One of the most recognizable lines from *Superman*, in all its various forms, is that guy yelling "Look, up in the sky! It's a bird! It's a plane! It's Superman!" But in the moment before it's made clear that Superman is flying by, doesn't the line imply that the guy's just some weirdo screaming at people to look at birds and planes all day?

Sincerely,

STEVE DELAHOYDE
CHICAGO, IL

DEAR MCSWEENEY'S,

For a time in my life, I worked in a chain bookstore. The chain no longer exists, but at the time it was the primary competition for the other really big chain bookstore that does still exist. One had to be swallowed for the other to survive, as is the way of things. I took the job because I was in my early twenties, and my mid-twenties were rapidly approaching, and I had nothing figured out. I'd quit my job working for the state of Ohio—a job I'd gotten only because my brother put in a good word for me—and had been spending my days in my apartment. An apartment that came with rent, which needed paying. An apartment that also was conveniently located directly next to a large chain bookstore.

I define most of my twenties by how little I was willing to move my body in order to obtain my needs and desires. This explains most of my friendships, relationships, and, of course, my employment. There was nothing I loved more than waking up at 8:45 for a shift beginning at nine, or having a resting place mere steps away after a day of standing. Some of my pals, then and now, still imagine that there are such things as "cool jobs," and I would like to say right here and now that this was not a cool job. I am too cynical, but there is no such thing as a cool job. Even as I write this, as a person in my thirties who lives my life as a writer, my e-mail inbox is an overgrown garden of anxieties and my calendar is flooding with red. I'm less interested in a cool job and more interested in a job that does not kill me, silently, from within.

At this chain bookstore, I was often relegated to the music section. This was during the last, loudly rattling moments of the CD era, and this bookstore had a robust CD section, peppered with a few records. It was a slightly adjusted version of a life-long dream I had of working in a record store. I had dreams of leaning over a counter while watching some suburban parents sift through the racks of music, asking me what I thought about the new Coldplay or the new Killers album, and I'd wave a dismissive hand and say, *Yeah, yeah, not bad, but it ain't like the old stuff, you know?*, and then I'd drop the needle on some Gladys or Otis or Aretha or some other shit like that. I wasn't (and am not) particularly a music snob in the strictest sense of the word, but I could play a convincing one, if the times demanded.

The problem was, most of the suburban shoppers at this bookstore didn't care much about opinions on music. They knew what they liked. They were there for books, and if they remembered or if the mood struck them, they'd come and snag a Norah Jones or Michael Bublé CD, and then keep it moving, oblivious to whatever musical vintage gold I'd strung along the music section's interior.

I remember the day I got the first phone call from someone who I'm going to call Steve, not because I'm changing his name, but because I genuinely never found out his name. He called to ask about some old Dream Theater CD—if I could order it and have it shipped directly to him. I could, so I did. During the filling out of the order sheet, we got to talking about Dream Theater. Steve was impressed to find out that I knew the band well, and wasn't just some kid, scraping some part-time coins together, pushing a few computer keys. After I got the order sent out, we talked for a few more minutes. About Rush, Yes, Gentle Giant, Opeth.

Steve would call every week or two and order a different CD. If I wasn't there, he'd leave a message for me, and I'd call him back when I got in. He'd ask for pressings of old Marvin Gaye albums or Emmylou Harris albums or Kinks albums, and we'd always stay on the phone, talking about the music he coveted, sometimes spiraling into a gentle debate about our favorite soul songs or whether or not rap music was a vital part of America's musical fabric. The place where I had his CDs shipped was close to the store, only a few blocks away. But he never came in, and I never asked why.

Steve's calls increased in frequency during the holiday season. He'd sometimes call twice a week. Our talks became longer, particularly if he called on a weeknight evening, when everything in the already-slow music section slowed even more. He seemed to understand that I was unfulfilled by the basic responsibilities of the job, and I seemed to understand that he was maybe unfulfilled by the silence of his own four walls. Judging from clues I picked up during our many talks, Steve was older than I was by at least three decades. He was a widower, and lived alone.

Around the first month of the next year, he stopped calling. I remember the last time we talked. Steve was on the hunt for a version of *Band on the Run*, and we talked for a while about McCartney, and grief, and loss. And then he was gone. He didn't call one week, and then the week turned into a month, and then another month, and then I slouched away from that job and sat in my lonely apartment for a few months, surrounded by my records.

I've been thinking about this thing that's been happening to me while I've been on my book tour, reading from and talking about a book that deals strictly with hip-hop. This thing where people, often white and often older, jump into the Q&A and try to stump me with their music knowledge, asking me about musicians they believe to be obscure. Or they will tire of the dialogue around hip-hop that I'm having with the audience and insert a question about some beloved rock band, thinking that I might not have the range to engage. Like all things that can be considered microaggressions, this act is entirely transparent to those subjected to it, and not as clever as the people engaging in the behavior think it is. I don't really mind this, and have gotten very accustomed to being able to pick out the (many) genuine, good-faith inquiries among the few bad-faith ones.

But I've been thinking about that year in my twenties, when I sat in a bookstore's CD section and talked to a man old enough to be my father about the music we both loved. I have been thinking about Steve, who knew I was young but talked to me with the assumption that I knew and understood music. And not just on the surface—all of the under-the-hood elements of it. I learned to be a critic from people like Steve, who chose to meet me where I was and talk to me about a shared passion. I'm so much more interested in that than I am in wielding information like a weapon. There was a real generosity in our talks that shaped how I talk to people about the things I love. An excitement, rooted in a desire to complete a bridge to each other.

I don't know what happened to Steve, and I have spent years trying not to think the worst. It was kind of a foolish exercise on its face, two strangers spending time on the phone for what must have amounted to tens of hours. I grew up talking music with strangers in chat rooms during the evolution of the internet, but I suppose the phone removes yet another barrier. Maybe

Steve just got his fill. Maybe his particular desire for another voice found a new home. But I think of him sometimes. Still living, I hope, streaming songs like the rest of us, with piles of CDs in an old box. Eventually, everything gets swallowed in the name of something else surviving.

Best,

HANIF ABDURRAQIB
COLUMBUS, OH

DEAR MCSWEENEY'S,

You know what else I love at a Q&A is when the person who stands up to ask a question is way more interested in showing the room how they know certain things and important people (basically nouns) than they are in getting their question answered.

Because one time I was splitting a turkey wrap with Mackenzie Phillips at this cafe (Mack's an old friend—she's such a lamb, only with a shocking incest history), and she told me about how, in France, they won't serve you a cappuccino after breakfast. I know what you're thinking! "Why not?" Because they are assholes.

JULIE KLAUSNER
NEW YORK, NY

from ISSUE 8

DEAR MCSWEENEY'S,

The greatest of all capers took place in high school. I'd been prac-
ticing my prank-calling since I was six years old. Two friends and
I once called the operator for hours, late into the night, until I went
and said something about tits. That comment got the operator mad,
and she called us back. The point is, I'd been doing this a while.
I knew how to keep it together. I never cracked a smile, or laughed.

We were on a big arts field trip to the ISAS arts festival in
Dallas. This was like a big high school art festival where we
did dance performances and took art classes and whatever else.
There were probably about a hundred kids from my school, and
about a hundred kids each from fifteen other Texas high schools.
It seemed like a lot of us were at the same motel.

I got on the phone and, with my friends Kerstin and Betsy
watching, I called the school valedictorian-to-be. She was in
room 324. I didn't really have a plan, but when she answered,
this perfect thing just unfolded itself.

"Room 224," I said, in a weary, tired voice, "I am tired of
the banging. I am tired of the screaming. I am tired of the
firecrackers and horsewhips—"

When she tried to interject, I spoke louder.

"I am exhausted, Room 224. It has been a long, long day. I do not want Room 224's excuses, I want its quiet."

I hung up. Then I waited about fifteen minutes and called again.

"Room 224. My children are awake. If your mission has been to awaken my children from their sleeping, then you have succeeded admirably. The baby is crying. He is hungry for milk. We are going down to Mexico to see the caves, as well as my husband, and we have been driving all day. Please, Room 224, do the right thing."

It went on like this a couple of rounds. I made the caller (me) seem like a wise and overworked waitress-type who was—somehow—repeatedly pushing the wrong buttons. Betsy and Kerstin did a lot of putting their hands over their mouths and throwing themselves into pillows. Somewhere in there, after four calls or so, we all headed over to the valedictorian-to-be's room.

"Guys!" she said, "This crazy lady is calling me. She keeps calling, complaining about Room 224 and cursing, but I called Room 224 and it was a family. I woke up a whole family!"

"You should get a teacher," I said. "Get Ms. Axelrod."

"Good idea," she said, "I will."

I have to say that I used to be a lot smoother and smarter than I am now. I really don't know how I had the balls to do this. You see, Ms. Axelrod was the video teacher, and I resented her. I resented her because I was accustomed to being the superstar in creative classes, and Ms. Axelrod didn't like me or my videos any more than she liked anybody else or their videos. I had a big head, still do.

Anyway, we went back to the room and called again. Stephanie answered. I knew Axelrod was in the room with her, and I heard the phone change hands, so I started cursing wildly, raving and screaming about the caves of Mexico and the firecrackers and the banging. After at least thirty seconds of concentrated insanity, I took a breath.

"Ma'am," Ms. Axelrod said, "You're speaking to a faculty member."

"Oh!" I gasped, and paused a second, as though centering myself. "I am so sorry. I would have never if I had known. You must forgive me, I—"

"You were speaking to one of my students. She was trying to sleep. You awoke her."

I couldn't believe it. There was no need to lie, here, I mean, Stephanie was being harassed and cursed at, so there was no call for saying she'd been woken up as well. In a way, it was great.

"I am so sorry, I didn't mean to wake her. I feel just awful, may I apologize?"

"Well, she's pretty sleepy."

"I'll just take one second, I want to tell her that I'm sorry…"

"Well… Okay." She handed the phone off.

"Hello?" Stephanie said.

What we're coming to now is one of my supremest and most glorious moments. I summoned up all my venom and hissed, "Why you little bitch."

Stephanie hung up. The next morning I slid into the bus seat behind Ms. Axelrod.

"Morning," I said. "Heard there was some trouble last night."

Axelrod told the story, but in her version, she came out like some sort of hero. Which makes me feel a little foolish. Not because I think her account is the correct one, but because her vanity makes my stomach hurt with how it resembles mine.

Sincerely,

AMIE BARRODALE
BROOKLYN, NY

RE:

DEAR MCSWEENEY'S,

I have a question that's not funny or particularly interesting, but I wanted to ask. I enjoy McSweeney's on the Web. I think it's funny. Sometimes I think, here are a bunch of people with my sense of humor, but sometimes it makes me worry. Do you (whoever's reading this) ever worry that you (personally, not as a magazine) place too much importance on irony/absurdity/cynicism? I think I may. I have a friend who told me that she almost cried during a movie because a scene was shot so beautifully, and I actually winced because she was so earnest. I have the same mixture of embarrassment and dread when a friend tells me that he/she writes poetry in his/her journal, horrified that I may be asked to read some of it. I used to think I was reacting against some sort of pretension, but these people are perfectly sincere. Then it occurred to me that I was reacting against their sincerity. I take very little seriously. My friends take very little seriously. Indeed, taking things too seriously (seriously at all) is grounds for being deemed pretty much unacceptable as companions, though perfectly nice people (also applies to people who pantomime golf swings). I get into this tricky spiral in which

I'm pretty sure I'm pretentious about being unpretentious, and it bugs me. I feel like I may not know the line between enjoying something because it is clever and enjoying it because it makes me feel clever. Does this ever bother you, reader mail-intake person? On second thought, it's probably just me. It usually is.

If I had the computer savvy to make this anonymous, I would have.

YUKIKO TAKEUCHI

DEAR MCSWEENEY'S,

I have long been meaning to bring this to your attention, but: as fine as your magazine is—and it is quite fine—there nevertheless seems to be something lacking: a mascot. All the great magazines have mascots. *Playboy,* of course, has its bowtie-wearing bunny—or "Geoffrey, the Fancy Rabbit," as I have named him. (I actually have developed a backstory for the *Playboy* bunny, available upon request.) The *New Yorker* has Eustace Tilley, the near-sighted lepidopterist, forever examining a butterfly atop the magazine's masthead. And *Ranger Rick* has Ranger Rick, the friendly raccoon. (Side note: did you know that raccoons are actually nocturnal animals, and, if you see one in the daylight, there's a decent chance that it has rabies? This bit of information sheds a whole new light on Ranger Rick, doesn't it? He's actually kind of a tragic figure, struggling just to get through the day and share his love of nature, all the while trying desperately not to think about how much he wants to bite someone's face off. He's like Edward from *Twilight,* but with a greater propensity toward marking his territory with glandular secretions.)

Those are just three examples of great magazines that have mascots. There are many, many others. *Mad* magazine, for instance. That's four.

So: where's your mascot? Lovely though your illustrations are, none of them cries out and says, "Yes! I am the embodiment of *McSweeney's*!" I have taken the liberty of coming up with a few possibilities for you. (Unfortunately, my drawing abilities are limited, but I can see each of them quite clearly in my head, and would be willing to work with a graphic artist to help realize my vision. Rest assured: I am not afraid to say "No, that's not it, try again!" as many times as it takes until the drawing resembles exactly what I imagine.)

Jim, the *McSweeney's* bird (he's wearing a cardigan sweater and he's got an air of erudition about him—he's lighting a pipe, and doing that thing that practiced pipe-smokers do, where they tilt their heads to one side and squint one eye as they light it, in order to keep the smoke out; obviously, there will be a disclaimer at the bottom, warning kids against the dangers of smoking)

Doug, the *McSweeney's* goat (he's standing on his hind legs, wearing overalls, winking and giving a thumbs-up, as if to say, "That's right, you know what I'm talking about!")

Harry Dean Stanton, the *McSweeney's* Harry Dean Stanton (it's just Harry Dean Stanton waving hello)

Those are just three suggestions—I have many more. Just let me know if you're interested, and I will get to work.

Sincerely,

TIM CARVELL
NEW YORK, NY

from ISSUE 54

DEAR MCSWEENEY'S,

This one time, I found a KFC logo on Google Earth. It was 2008 and I was trying to look at Area 51 in Nevada (just like probably a million other people). If not paranormal, it was definitely abnormal, this aproned colonel smiling into outer space. Most of all, I was unsettled by the logo's sharpness compared to the dusty desert surrounding it. It almost looked like an icon, but when I tried to click on it, nothing happened.

I googled "KFC google earth" and found a press release. Apparently, years earlier, KFC had unveiled what it claimed was the world's first "astrovertisement"—a giant logo made of sixty-five thousand red, white, and black plastic tiles. Strangely, the press release (now gone) was written in the UK, so they kept comparing its size to British things like Stonehenge and Big Ben. "The largest stones in Stonehenge are the Sarsen stones which measure 8ft wide by 25ft long," they wrote. "Based on this measurement, you would be able to fit 435 stones into the KFC logo."

Fifty people took three weeks to arrange the tiles. If you search "KFC face from space" on YouTube you will find a very satisfying time-lapse video of the Colonel being assembled row by row, with some cars and a few portable toilets off to the side. They start from the bottom of the logo, so it looks like an upside-down version of a JPEG loading in 1995. At the end, the toilets disappear and all of the cars drive away.

The video convinced me that, indeed, the Colonel's image was affixed not to a picture of the Earth, but to the Earth itself. Well, sort of. By the time I saw it, it was actually gone from physical reality, having been removed six months after it was installed. During those six months, someone in Rachel, Nevada, might have walked out of the Area 51-themed Little A'Le'Inn and seen a meaningless sea of plastic tiles. Then some people (the same people?) came and took the plastic tiles away. Yet here I was, looking at them. I was reminded of the feeling I have when I look at the stars, knowing that what I'm seeing is out of date.

Honestly, though, this slippage between past and present was something I was used to as a Google Earth addict. It seems a bit smoother now, but back then Google Earth was made up of patches taken from noticeably different sources at different times. Hence the places where Interstate 80 would pass abruptly from a dry summer to the whitest of winters, lakes that were half empty and half full, and cities whose shadows fell in two different directions. I'd already begun to ascribe to these places some kind of reality of their own. Having initially gone to Google Earth for a picture of my physical world, I found instead another world—a patchy, mysterious, time-warping one with partial seasons and logos that linger indefinitely. The time in which I flew over the patchwork mountains was its own time, outside of the time of the map.

So it didn't matter to me that the Colonel wasn't really there anymore. And it certainly didn't matter to KFC! The logo was built to be seen from space, to be registered by a satellite. You could say that the minute it was launched into visibility by Google Earth, its persistence on the ground became merely incidental.

Then, years after disappearing from the ground, the logo disappeared from Google Earth. I first noticed this in 2014. At the intersection of Old Mill Road and Groom Road, there were now just some mysterious and unreadable squiggles. Why did it make me sad? I don't even like KFC—I'm pescatarian. Maybe it was just the reminder that these days a lot of things disappear not once but twice.

I'm looking at the spot now, and I notice that later in 2014, someone named Junxiao Shi made a photosphere (a 360-degree panorama) in front of the Little A'Le'Inn. I pick up my Pegman, dangle him over the photosphere's blue circle, and drop into the map. In the blinding sunlight, an old man in khakis is walking toward the motel. In map time, he will always be walking— walking and walking, and never getting there. I scroll 180 degrees to face the former site of the Colonel. I zoom in. I see nothing but a few small signs and, in the distance, purple mountains dissolving into pixels. I wonder if they still look that way.

Ever yours,

JENNY ODELL
OAKLAND, CA

DEAR MCSWEENEY'S,

While I was in college, I had to take a world geography class for a required elective. One day we discussed the equator and I was reminded of a girl with whom I graduated from high school. In seventh grade, while coincidentally also in a geography class, the said girl raised her hand and asked if the equator was an actual line drawn across the world with a Sharpie. As an addendum, she asked about the upkeep of such a line. In tribute to my theory that the truly ignorant are the only pure form of entertainment left in the world, I raised my hand in the five-hundred-person lecture and asked the girl's complete question, addendum included.

I ain't got no pride,

COLE WALTER

from ISSUE 47

DEAR MCSWEENEY'S,

When I was in eighth grade, one of our assignments for English class was to give a five-minute speech. I think the point was to make us feel comfortable speaking in front of other people. Mr. Johnson (author of *Improve Your Own Spelling* and *Love and Sex in Plain Language*, the latter of which analyzed the ovaries with intense specificity while withholding the least piece of useful information about the meaning of "sixty-nine") encouraged us not to worry about *what* we planned to talk about, but *how* we planned to speak. I can't remember my speech; I'm sure I was nervous. I was a very nervous girl—"high-strung," as our next-door neighbor, who also happened to be the family pediatrician, unkindly put it. What I do remember is the speech given by one of the twin boys in my class— the one in my section, not the one who got expelled for shooting off a cap pistol in Quaker meeting. The speech focused on the different kinds of sidewalk he encountered while walking home from school. Relying heavily on the obsessively repeated phrase "and then," Charles's speech described, in excruciating detail, sections of concrete, some with cracks having weeds growing out of them and some not; sections of brickwork, some in a herringbone pattern and some not; huge slabs of slate, most of them cracked; random patches of dirt; outcroppings of moss…

Really, I remember an astonishing amount of the twin's speech, especially given how boring it was. I remember nothing—I repeat, *nothing*—about any of the other speeches.

I think of this as the "no stone left unturned" school of narrative. (The girl was putting on her coat. She was buttoning the buttons. She was putting on her boots and walking across the living-room rug to the front door. She was opening the door. She was closing it behind her. She was turning the key in the lock…) Several nights ago at dinner a poet friend urged her husband—engaged in telling a story about the wild early days of the cooking school he founded—to skip over the boring background material. "You were sitting in your second-floor office. You looked out the window and saw…" She leaned forward and made a hurry-up-and-tell-the-story gesture. Meanwhile her husband proceeded, undeterred. There was crucial information we needed in order to understand what he was about to say, despite the fact that the poet—in the time-honored manner of poets—was suggesting the benefits of narrative compression and an attendant use of bold transitions.

What is a transition, exactly? It's the place where we're in transit. A mysterious place, as in the transit from life to death. What goes on there?

I thought of this recently, when I was on an airplane. It was an overbooked flight, meaning we were all crammed into the plane together, whether we liked it or not. Why did I not want to talk to the person next to me? I'm sure the fear-of-boringness factor played a part, but I'm also pretty sure that wasn't the chief reason. In fact, my seatmate looked like an interesting-enough person and—once he'd initiated a conversation—turned out to be just that, a doctor who had spent his last ten days doing humanitarian work in Haiti.

When I was eight years old I spent three weeks in the hospital after a tine test for tuberculosis came back positive. This was the early fifties, and while a successful treatment for the disease existed, my parents were both traumatized, the diagnosis having been delivered with what I am certain was a degree of satisfaction by the pediatrician next door. Years later my father confessed that he was afraid I was going to die an "endless, noisy death," as he put it, like the consumptive heroines of the operas my mother enjoyed listening to on Saturday afternoons. Neither of them explained why I needed to be sent to the hospital, only that I was going in for "tests." Of course, like any high-strung girl born into a repressed fifties household, I was adept at reading clues. The sighs. The exchanged looks. The dish of fruit Jell-O deposited on my hospital bed tray, followed by the unnaturally speedy exit. My parents knew I was dying and were trying to wean themselves of their attachment to me.

Those three weeks, then, were a kind of transition—it was as if I was in a place where I already knew I wasn't *there*. A place between life and death, though I'd never have put it that way. I remember riding the elevator down to the basement with the very cute boy whose bed was directly across from mine in the children's ward—we both had to be x-rayed on a regular basis. The x-ray was clearly a kind of test, one that both of us were failing. Where were we really, though? The bardo?

Before I went into the hospital I'd coveted a doll dressed in a bridal gown you could see when you looked through the heart-shaped cellophane opening in the lid of the box she came in. This was before Barbie; the doll was smaller but also, like Barbie, blond, with pixie features, a face about as much unlike mine as a face could be. I forget who it was who brought me the doll. I don't think it was either of my parents; it might have been a neighbor. I received quite a lot of presents during my hospital stay, including a weird succulent in a bird-shaped planter and a beautiful illustrated edition of *The Adventures of Robin Hood*. If a present came wrapped, I must have removed the wrapping paper, but that was where my engagement with it ended. The doll stayed in her box: I never undid the little wires attaching her to the box at the wrists and ankles. It was as if, during those three weeks, time ceased to exist, and with it, life.

Exactly like what happens on an airplane.

Being on a plane is like being in the bardo. You aren't *anywhere*. Unlike in the twin's meticulous description of his journey from school to home, every footstep accounted for, you leave accountable space behind. And yet why should it be the case that in both instances the experience is one of boredom?

Last summer, with my friends Steve and Sabrina, I walked a section of the famous pilgrim trail that begins in a host of different places but always ends at Santiago de Compostela, home to the earthly remains of the apostle James. In France the trail is called Le Chemin; we started our walk in Le Puy (a volcanic landscape that also happens to be the lentil capital of the world) and ended in the village of Flaujac (where in the twenties my friend Sabrina's artist grandparents built a house).

I remember, before starting out, standing atop an impossibly old magma plug called the Needle. The morning was beautiful, the streets of Le Puy empty of all but a few clerics in long black cassocks, sliding along the steep pathways like chessmen. Dew had fallen on everything, leaving behind the smell of wet stone and, as the sun rose, the smell of water evaporating. This could happen to you, I told myself. You could evaporate. It hadn't always been the case that there were trail blazes to guide an errant pilgrim—in the Middle Ages many pilgrims got lost, never to be seen again, especially while navigating Domaine du Sauvage, a stretch of Le Chemin known for its wild beasts and terrible weather, its hail and lightning and impenetrable fog.

Even though the volcano that exploded where I stood had been asleep for centuries, I could feel, coming up through the bottoms of my feet and out through the top of my head, the insane fury of the Earth's molten core. Before it had been a shrine to Saint Michael, this had been a shrine to Mercury, god of messages and poetry, commerce and thieves. He was also charged with conveying the souls of the newly dead to the Underworld. Little green lizards suddenly appeared from between crevices in the stonework and just as suddenly disappeared back into them, their pink tongues poking in and out of their sly, grinning mouths.

Best,

KATHRYN DAVIS
MONTPELIER, VT

DEAR MCSWEENEY'S,

I'll give you this: sunny as it was, that day in Anderson's field may have been just a day. But there were more like it. A lot more.

When Rabs and me were fifteen, my little brother Jonathan got a green and yellow parakeet. I wanted to name it Motorbike, but since it was Jonathan's bird, and since he was only four, we ended up calling it Pedro the Parrot.

Rabs was furious. He came straight over, walked up to Jonathan, and demanded an audience. They met in Jonathan's room.

Since I wasn't invited, and since they closed the door, I can't tell you exactly what was said. Still, with an ear pressed to the thin bathroom wall, I can give you the gist of it. There are over three hundred types of parrots.

"If Pedro should have a last name at all, it should be Parakeet." I heard Rabs yell. "Or better yet, Budgerigar."

Rabs had a point. It turns out that "Pedro the Parrot" was even more than a parakeet, he was a particular kind of parakeet. Pedro was a budgerigar.

It's too bad this bit of ornithology didn't impress Jonathan, because Rabs didn't give up. He started coming over every night after dinner just to lecture Jonathan. It got to the point where if you wanted to find Rabs, you'd look in Jonathan's room first. More often than not he'd be there, pointing at some picture, book, or bar graph while little Jonathan sat, legs dangling from the edge of his bed.

They'd be at it for hours. Sometimes mom had to kick Rabs out so Jonathan could get some sleep. Before he would leave, though, Rabs always extended his hand to Jonathan and asked for Pedro to be renamed. Jonathan would shake that hand and his own head simultaneously.

A year passed before this stalemate was finally broken. On Pedro's birthday, we liberated him from his cage and he flew straight for the bay window in my family room. Before Rabs showed up for cake, Jonathan had me cross out REEBOK and write PEDRO THE PARROT on the coffin.

Rabs took it hard. He told me he never wanted to hear the name Pedro the Parrot again. If I thought he'd listen, I'd have told him what my mom let me in on earlier that day. Apparently, Jonathan knew all along that Pedro was more than a parrot. He just couldn't pronounce *parakeet,* let along *budgerigar.* He was only four.

Sincerely,

TREVOR KOSKI
CHICAGO, IL

from ISSUE 48

DEAR MCSWEENEY'S,

When I was twelve years old, my family and I moved into a new house that had a fifty-gallon fish tank embedded in a wall. One side of the tank could be seen from the hallway; the other side faced my mother's desk in the kitchen. We'd had a small freshwater fish tank at the old house, with little pebbles at the bottom and darting neon fish, but this new tank was four times as big, and would be filled with saltwater.

My dad ordered "live rock"—porous rocks from the ocean floor, made up of dead coral that contained algae, microorganisms, sponges, and snails. These rocks give a tank a readymade ecosystem of plants and tiny creatures, while also stabilizing the water chemistry. My dad piled them up in the tank, creating a network of hidden paths and hiding places. I would sit in a rolly chair with a magnifying glass, examining the growing number of little tubes pressed against the glass, trying to discern if they were plants or animals.

My dad ordered fish, too, and hermit crabs, jumbo snails, clams, shrimp, and sea anemones. The clown fish fed and tended to their anemones. Cleaner shrimp swayed side to side under their rocks; one time I saw them cleaning a clown fish's teeth. There was a red-banded coral shrimp, Sylvester, with six-inch antennae, who would always hang upside down beneath a rock of his own, his razor-sharp claws outstretched, waiting.

We had two hermit crabs—Rocky and Hermie. Rocky often had flowing green algae growing from his shell, and once we saw Hermie riding on top of him, eating the algae. We were so drawn to these creatures that when, one day, my mom and I spotted Rocky's shell perched on the highest rock, the remains of his body below him, we mourned his death. It was hours before we learned that Rocky had just shed his skin, a typical phase in his growth. Every few months, the hermit crabs did this. We called Hermie's shed skin his "pajamas," because that's what it looked like—orange stripes on reddish orange.

There were always new things going on. Beautiful "feather duster" tube worms unfurled like ornate fans. Home from school one day, I got to witness a snail give birth against the glass. My favorite creature was something we called the Green Pancake, which slowly traveled the rocks. The Green Pancake had a whitish base and a green dimpled platform top that contorted with the creature's mood. An anemone crab the size of a penny rode this Pancake around, pawing at the air with two webbed claws.

Tragedy often befell the tank. There was a fish named Hawk, who was red and sort of reptilian—his fins were separated like fingers, his eyes rotated to all angles, and he perched on particular rocks for long periods of time before scurrying off. Hawk always minded his own business, and often roosted on Dad's fingers when he fed the fish from a block of frozen shrimp. When Hawk died, my parents replaced him with another, almost identical fish, a spotted Hawk, except this Hawk was evil and killed most of the other fish. We would see Sylvester the shrimp eating their remains.

Throughout the ongoing drama of the fish tank—who was attacking who, which corals were struggling—there were brief, startling glimpses of a creature we had not purchased. The creature was a sectioned worm with hundreds of leglike protrusions and an iridescent sheen. It was as fat as my thumb, and we never saw its full body. It had six antennae and a big, smiling mouth. We called it Smiley. When it didn't react to our flashlight, we decided it was blind.

Smiley ate massive amounts of algae. Since we didn't see him eat the shrimp my dad occasionally fed the fish, we concluded that Smiley was a vegetarian. Months would go by without a Smiley spotting, and then he'd appear, extending slowly out of the rocks, taking in a mouthful of sand. He was my favorite part of the tank and the greatest mystery of my young existence. Sometimes we saw dark gray egg-shaped deposits that we guessed were Smiley's poops. These were lightweight and swayed with the water. We called them "movin' poops."

Over the years, Smiley became more brazen. By the time he began emerging while my dad fed the fish, we had seen at least ten inches of him, and had been appalled and amazed that, as I put it, Smiley "had hands in his mouth"—black, handlike jaws that grabbed things and pulled them into his mouth. The other fish were diminishing, and we suspected that Smiley was eating them.

My friend Joe did some research. The internet claimed that Smiley was a pest, and that no creature or plant could survive in a tank with him. The easiest way to catch him, according to the message boards, was to take a plastic container and cut an X in its lid. Then you were meant to push the points of the X inward, and put food in the container. Smiley would go for the food and get speared by the plastic points of the X, after which he could be removed from the tank by gloved hands. His skin was poisonous. I liked Smiley far too much to ever tell my dad about this.

But fish kept dying. The sea anemones shrank and withered. A crazy hermit crab named Chip grew surprisingly fast and began attacking the feather dusters and anything else that moved. When my dad reached into the tank to grab Chip, the crab abandoned his shell and ran naked into the rocks. When I mentioned Smiley at a fish store, they advised me to capture him immediately.

And so we placed the trap in the tank. Smiley had stripped all the rocks of algae by then, and few fish remained. Where there had once been colorful, gleaming, spectacular creatures, there was now bare rock and this bizarre sea worm, who slunk mannerless behind the rocks and made slimy tunnels in the sand. He wouldn't go near the plastic container.

My dad grew frustrated. It was declared that after the last fish died, the rocks would be removed, the water drained, and the tank filled with fresh water. I was very opposed to this, but by then I was out of college and not living nearby. The only fish that remained were one damselfish—just a small blue body and yellow tail, who had lived in the tank for a least a decade and did nothing of note—and the latest Hawk fish, who had the exact characteristics of the first Hawk.

One day, on a visit home, my parents told me Smiley had died, and that the dead body was visible. I looked, and it was true. A portion of Smiley lay outside of the rocks, but as before, I still couldn't see the whole length. I stood with my flashlight, examining the scene. Glumly, I studied the remaining algae on the glass. After a moment, I saw them—teeny worms! There were colonies of them between the glass and the algae, visible only to a squinting, longing eye.

Some segmented sea worms, it turns out, reproduce asexually. They die, and from each segment of their body hatch their offspring. Our tank was full of Baby Smileys. I watched over them with my magnifying glass; my friend Noah wanted us to raise them, then travel the country selling them to aquariums. But the next day my dad cleaned the tank walls with a razor (as he had always done), and to my horror clumps of Baby Smileys were sent to choke on air in the compost pile in our yard.

There may still be young Smileys hidden in the tank, catching things with the black hands of their mouths, but I haven't been able to spot one in years. Hawk is the last fish standing, swimming around by himself, delaying the freshwater transition, while algae grows thick on the walls.

Through the years I've told this story to friends, presenting a photo I took of Smiley in the late nineties. My boyfriend is afraid of the photo, which adds to Smiley's undying power. All the narratives and beauties of the tank—the mandarin fish with its frog face, paisley-print body, and fluttery, gauzelike fins; the strange, puffy brain coral—are eclipsed by this sand monster. Every few months a news story about a weird aquarium creature is posted online, and friends of mine send me the link, always prefacing it with a question: "Smiley?"

Yours,

RACHEL B. GLASER
NORTHAMPTON, MA

DEAR KEVIN,

Correct me if I'm wrong, but I also hear you saying that people who have sudden and sympathetic emotional reactions to lost cats and dogs may, in fact, make better readers of your fiction than people who, say, walk into a bookstore expressly looking to pass their eyes over some fiction. Why is that?

EDITOR

DEAR EDITOR,

Not better readers, but different ones. Let's say we conducted the experiment in a different way. Suppose I created this story as described, but instead of posting it myself, around my neighborhood, you published it here, with a note on the facing page suggesting that readers make copies of the piece and put them up around their hometown. Now, in *McSweeney's*, it would appear as a short story written on a piece of paper that looks a little like a cat poster. That's precious. But if one reader tacks it up on a telephone poll, in Tampa or Toronto or wherever, it becomes a short story *pretending* to be a cat poster, and it will be read by passerby with a completely different set of eyes. An individual who first encounters the story here, where one would expect to see fiction and mischief and literary games and so forth, could never have the same reaction to it as a person who first encounters it on the street.

Here's a barely related thought: In Chicago, no one visits the Art Institute without marveling at the Chagall or the Seurat, but I bet virtually all of those people, on the way back to their cars, would walk right past the Gamera-sized Picasso in Daley Plaza and not even think to look up.

KEVIN GUILFOILE
CHICAGO, IL

DEAR MCSWEENEY'S,

It's been a few weeks now and I have not yet received word back from you re: Helen Hunt's grandmother's coconut-macaroon recipe. It's possible I was not entirely clear in my original letter: please do not respond only if the interview was published in your quarterly; I need to hear from you either way. And, if you have access to *Redbook*'s archives through some sort of magazine-publishing database, please also send me a copy. All my best,

JEN STATSKY
NEW YORK, NY

P.S. Please read the interview in its entirety before you send it to make sure it is the one where Helen Hunt gives her grandmother's coconut-macaroon recipe and not some other interview where she does not. She seems like the type who gives a lot of interviews.

DEAR MCSWEENEY'S,

I live in St. Paul, Minnesota. A nice place where God tries to ice-murder all inhabitants every year. If you survive, you have defeated God, so that gives you a nice boost of confidence heading into springtime.

On a recent spring day, I took two of my three kids to see a Minnesota Timberwolves basketball game. I encourage my kids to follow the exploits of the Timberwolves—they can be very instructive. The Timberwolves' players are not generally all that interested in playing basketball, and you get the sense that they are only playing the game to get a little exercise so that when they adjourn to play Xbox for the rest of the night they won't feel so guilty. I tell my kids not to make the wrong choices in life or they could end up playing for the Timberwolves themselves. I did not take the third child to the game, because she is too young to be exposed to such things.

Prior to the game, we decided to stop for dinner at the Subway restaurant on Fairview and Grand Avenue in St. Paul. You know the one. It's by the movie theater and kitty-corner from Whole Foods. We like Subway. My son gets the meatball sub so he can drip sauce on his shirt and look like a slob all day. My daughter enjoys a turkey sandwich so bereft of additional ingredients that it's a crime to pay what I do for it.

After she ordered her turkey sandwich, I thought turkey sounded pretty good too. So here's what I did: I ordered a turkey sandwich with Havarti cheese. Turkey and Havarti. One of my favorite combinations. Can't go wrong. A sure-fire winner.

But the order did not fire sure. It was not a winner. "Turkey and *what?*" asked the incredulous sandwich artist.

"Turkey and... Havarti? You don't have Havarti, do you?"

"I don't even know what you're talking about!" she said with kind of a chuckle. "That's not a real thing, is it?"

"Of course it's a real thing," I stammered. "It's Havarti cheese. It's creamy and delicious and goes well with turkey."

"*Havarti?*" she asked, turning to her fellow sandwich artists, who offered only confused expressions and shakes of the head.

She thought this: I had entered a Subway with two young kids, decided to make up a complete nonsense word, and pretended that it was a form of cheese. This, deduced the sandwich artist, was a choice I had made.

McSweeney's, have you ever been in a situation where you're telling the truth but someone doesn't believe you? And the more you insist on the truth, the more it sounds like you're lying? This was me. I had to defend Havarti's existence. But it's as if I was defending a legitimately fictitious cheese. "Do you have any Blamptonshire cheese? How about Flogvers? Or a lovely slice of Greevenheimer?"

It was at this point that I thought about hauling the kids across the intersection to Whole Foods, where I'm sure Havarti could be had, and buying a slice just to bring back. I might have even done it. I'm kind of a jerk like that. But then I worried that maybe I was a snob. I never thought of Havarti as being an elite cheese, a cheese for the cheese cognoscenti—but did I truly understand what made a cheese elite, McSweeney's?

A Subway is a hell of a place to have an existential crisis. I told them fine, pepper jack. Whatevs, you know?

We went to the Timberwolves game and they lost badly to the Phoenix Suns as thousands of Minnesotans watched. It was a grim, self-flagellating exercise.

Okay then, McSweeney's. Bye. I love you.

JOHN MOE
ST. PAUL, MN

from ISSUE 37

DEAR MCSWEENEY'S,

While dining recently at a Mexican cantina in Atlanta, I had a nice chat with L. (male) and A. (female). They are one of my favorite couples in the world, only in part because they are so much younger than me. I am but a gritty old weed next to their flourishing promise and gumption, which smells, at least on the lovely A., like something that blossoms pinkish-purplish. As a weed, I like sucking up what they have to say.

Our discussion turned to various things having to do with love. As of this writing, L. and A. have been dating a long while. They are not yet engaged, but you know the deal: if they don't make it happen soon, their families and friends will step in.

On this night, they talked about another couple they knew, who were planning a wedding. There was to be a bachelor party in Rio during Carnaval and a bachelorette party in Sonoma. I've been married before, and mahogany, the money that's thrown at weddings, you know? L. and A., however, felt no obligation to compare their future nuptials to others'. It heartened me, to see them unperturbed.

The conversation then veered toward A.'s recent trip home

to Chicago, where she met up at a bar with her "first love" and "first sexual partner" (the same man). He brought along a female friend, a scientist from Greece. They all got on really well, A. said.

McSweeney's, there is no observer on the planet that could look at A. and not think, "Criminy, that is one pretty girl." The curly hair, the fresh face—it's undeniable. Slathered over the top of all this is a daring, intellectual personality. And as A. relayed this story, I felt myself thinking, my mind crimped in a defensive posture for L., "Yeah, well, it's no mystery what the guy was hoping for."

A. continued. She and her former lover had told their relationship story to the scientist: how they had fallen for each other, how they had had fun sex, how they had stayed together for years too long. And the scientist asked, "Why aren't you still together?"

Here I looked at L. and thought, "You are better than me, sitting there so calmly."

But A. finished by saying how healthy it was to sit with an old beau and explain to someone (a scientist, no less) why they'd broken up. So, I thought, this is what people do now with their exes. I felt inspired by it.

Next it was L.'s turn. As it happens, the girl he had dated in high school had fatefully stepped into the same Mexican cantina where we presently dined. She was across the room. He hadn't seen her in years. She was on crutches. He would say hello to her later. I don't know if there is symbolism in this. But her presence opened the doors to a story.

Their relationship had fallen apart, of course—college, craziness. But L. remembered fondly how he used to sneak over to this girl's house and stand outside her window, waiting for a hookup session. (A. seemed to really enjoy this part; I don't know how these kids are so healthy.) You are familiar with this romantic setting.

This is when I, the out-of-touch weed, jumped in. "Let me

guess—you'd throw a rock against her window? And she'd sneak you in?"

L. looked perplexed. The needle scratched on the record. A. turned to me and said, "Wait, you've actually thrown *rock*s against someone's *window*?"

Then L., attempting to help, hoisted his cell phone. "Well, no, actually," he said. "I had one of these." L. and A. chuckled knowingly.

And my very first thought was, You threw your *cell phone* at her window?

But no, thankfully, I did not say that, and anyway L. made a gesture that indicated he had used the cell phone to contact his temporary sweetheart from outside her window and arranged the make-outs.

Call me old-fashioned, but this information floored me. I didn't have a cell phone in high school. I'm almost completely sure they weren't invented yet. We only had pebbles and rocks and sticks to conjure love. Which is why I'm writing.

We live in fast times, we all agree. Emotional maturity may well be at an all-time high. But let us stop a moment to record this: sometime in the last ten to fifteen years, the act of using a pebble and a window to woo a high-school hookup passed from literal practice into the figurative, irresponsible-seeming sort. Try a rock on a window now, and the object of your affection will probably just respond with an angry text.

For an old weed like me, it's difficult to keep up.

Yours,

JAMIE ALLEN
ATLANTA, GA

DEAR McSWEENEY'S,

My cousin is in her first year at Harvard Medical School, and my mother raised me, so you can imagine how much weight their advice carries. Recently they both mentioned, independent of each other, that I should get a physical. Both were disappointed that I couldn't remember when I'd last had one. My guess was I'd gone before I started college; otherwise I wouldn't have been allowed to move into the dorms, right?

I ended up looking online for providers, and found one so close to my house that I would most likely not be late to my appointment. That's how I chose my doctor. It's probably my fault the visit was atrocious.

When I called up to set a visit, I was informed that, as a new patient, there would be no physical exam during the initial appointment. It would only be a meet-and-greet; the doctor and I would be there to establish our relationship.

Weirdly refreshing, I thought to myself. What a throwback to a simpler, less extortionist time! I've heard so much about how impersonal doctor visits are these days; I had been prepared for the cold, five-minute in-and-out. Somehow, it seemed, my search engine had scuttled past everything that is wrong with our health care system.

Appointment day arrived. The doctor came in upbeat and very engaged, tricking me. She patted my knee as she walked by—which I appreciated, but now see as a harbinger of the death of the Hippocratic oath. She looked at me so avidly my gaze dropped to the floor.

"So, how did you hear about me?" she said.

Her face was expectant, poised to (I'm pretty sure) receive notice of glowing referrals. I readjusted my position in my chair.

"Uh, the provider list," I said. "This office is really close to my house."

She nodded in swift hiccups. She said, "So none of your friends go to me?" Her face was still open, but straining. At this point I was compelled to manage her feelings, because sometimes I am very compassionate.

I said, "Well, they definitely could, but we don't really talk about our doctors."

I couldn't tell if this made her feel better, but she moved on.

She asked, "So do you need an STD screening?"

"No, I'm good on all that, thanks," I said. "Just went to the gynecologist last month."

She looked down at her clipboard. "Okay, but, just so you know, I do all that stuff. It's my field. I mean, I teach at universities, I'm on panels. It's kind of my thing."

"Oh," I said. "That's great."

"Yeah, it's definitely my thing. You could come to me with any questions, or tests you need to get done... So who's your gyno?"

"You know," I said. "I can't quite remember the name. They were on the provider list."

"Okay. Well, you can do all that with me from now on. I'm, you know, you can come to me. I do it all."

"Okay," I said, "sure, yes. Streamlining. Sure." Faint alarms buzzed in my mind. But I am naive and a pleaser, so I stayed supportive of her and second-guessed myself. I couldn't remember what it was like to see a general practitioner. Maybe they always tried to be your gynecologist as well?

She skimmed the forms I had filled out. "Well, you seem very healthy," she said. "You're in a relationship? That lowers your risk factors." She looked at me a long while. Instinctively, I started to squirm. "Well. Now I'm looking at your face. What's that, that blemish? Does that happen when you get your period?"

"Yes, sometimes," I said, trying to hide my chin from her.

"Have you ever been on birth control?"

"What? Um, yes."

"But you're not now?"

"Well, I had weird reactions to it. And—"

"You should get on birth control. It will regulate your hormones."

"Riiiiight," I said, truly confused now. "But... I'm sorry, what are we talking about?"

"Everything is a matter of hormones," she said. "They just need to be regulated."

"Okay, yes, but I think I'm doing an okay job on my own." I tried a slow smile to show that I was open to suggestions, yet incredibly self-assured.

"Do you cramp a lot on your period?"

"No, I don't," I said. The alarms were getting louder.

"Well, on birth control you would cramp even less. You could get the ring; you could go all year without having a period. There is no [here she made finger quotation marks] 'need to bleed.' As a matter of fact, as recently as two hundred years ago, you would spend years and years not bleeding, because you would be pregnant the entire time."

I wanted the tiny hammer on my kneecaps; I wanted to see a stethoscope. I did not want to hear any more talk about the bleeding of frontier women.

But she was still talking.

"There are things we inherit, no use questioning it. Me, I'm fifty years old and I have not one gray hair on my head. Because of my father. You, you're almost thirty, and look." She pointed to my chin. "That's probably because of your parents. It's all hormones. So, you want to leave here with a prescription?"

At that instant I had a fantasy: I was meeting her for the first time at a dinner party, learning what she did for a living, absorbing her personality, and then walking away, forever, grateful she wasn't my doctor.

"No, thank you," I said. "I'm okay for now."

She was looking at what I assume was a checklist. "Have you ever had depression?"

"No," I lied.

"Both your parents healthy?"

"Yes, I guess."

"You see both your parents?"

"Um, just my mom, mostly."

"What happened to your dad?"

"My dad? He and I don't talk that much."

"Are you in therapy?"

I panicked. I had to derail her. I asked, "What about skin cancer? Can you check me for skin cancer? I know this isn't the exam part, but my cousin said I should get my moles checked for skin cancer."

"Okay, well, sure, I can check," she said. "Do you have moles you want me to look at?"

I scanned my arms and legs for anything. "No, but maybe on my back? I can't see my back."

She told me to get on the exam table. She started checking my back. I thought, This feels more normal. Now she was acting like a doctor. In my mind I chanted: *Shhh, shhh, don't talk, don't talk.*

"All clear!" she said. "No moles."

I was putting my shirt back on, brainstorming something to mumble as I fled.

"Well," she was saying, "I know this might not come up for you, but just so you know…"

My breath caught. I couldn't possibly know.

"I do abortions. Right here, in this office. You could get one here, if you ever needed to."

I made a long humming noise and tapped my right thumb, which is what I do when a doctor tries to sell me a future abortion.

"I'm very active with reproductive rights. I've served on a lot of panels. I've written about it, I teach. I'm really strong in the field. You should come to me, if you ever, you know."

I sat on the edge of the exam table, legs swinging.

"I mean, you never know what could happen. You said you tour, right? So. I'm here. And your friends, you could let them know, too."

I nodded once, exhaled. Yes, I could.

She smiled at me. "Just in case. I'll be here." She stood and took my hand. "It was so great to meet you."

She walked me out and asked the receptionist to schedule me for the physical. I tried to tell the receptionist "NO!" with my eyes, but nothing transmitted. I canceled the next day.

Now I have a different doctor. And yes, they're in the same office. I know, I know. It's just… They're so close to my house.

THAO NGUYEN
SAN FRANCISCO, CA

DEAR MCSWEENEY'S,

This is a strange pet peeve to have, but I'll say it anyway: the Jonestown Massacre involved Flavor Aid. Not Kool-Aid. It's true. So, from now on, whenever you hear someone say, "Hey, I bet that [so and so] drank the Kool-Aid," I'd like for you to do the following: take that person gently by the elbow, lead him or her to a quiet spot, and then (without malice) say, "It was actually Flavor Aid, not Kool-Aid. An entirely different brand. Okay?" Then lead him or her gently back to the conversation and make sure that before you leave, you hear them say: "Hey, I bet that [so and so] drank the Flavor Aid." Smile. Nod. Walk away. Job well done, sir.

MIKE SACKS
POOLESVILLE, MD

DEAR EDITOR,

The subway in Santiago seems like it's new, but new from the mid-seventies. Like someone got it as a model kit for Christmas in 1977, along with a shiny satin baseball jacket and some *Star Wars* action figures but then stuffed it in the back of the closet until he stumbled on it last year and decided it might still work. And then he put together and laid it out, life-size, underneath the city where the smoke is so bad it turns white shirts gray in a matter of hours. The *Star Wars* action figures would be at home in the Santiago subway system; the stations are huge and hangar-like; they are concrete and orange and often empty; the escalators and revolving doors move noiselessly, as if transporting ghosts. Everything feels like a futurist's prediction that hasn't aged well. The subway in Santiago has promotional posters that advertise its stations as "Our New Cathedrals," a slogan which is only funny if you picture the ambitious bureau-crats who came up with it, seated around table after one of the two- or three-hour lunches that are the norm here. It's funny only if you picture them really trying to come up with the perfect catch phrase, something that would really make people appreciate these monuments to efficiency and mobility, these public places that the public doesn't visit but merely moves through. It's funny only if you picture these men turning the thought ("Cathedrals, yes, *cathedrals*") over in their minds as they drive home to the suburbs whose names, to my California ears, give the city an unearned familiarity: Los Condes, Bellavista, Rio Maipo. It's funny only if you picture these men taking off their shoes as they get ready for bed, the soot and dust of the city still clinging to their socks, to the hairs on the back of their hands, and to their eyelashes as they close their lids and begin to dream of the empty cavern beneath them, flooded with fluorescent light and silence.

ANA MARIE COX
SAN FRANCISCO, CA

from ISSUE 44

DEAR MCSWEENEY'S,

I have come, a recalcitrant thirty-six-year-old mom, to Des Moines, Iowa, which is like America's dream of an America where no Kennedys ever died. The best coffee shop has a flavor called "Jamaican Me Crazy."

"Is Iowa in the United States?" asks my older son, strapped securely behind me in our car seat–laden Suby. Yes, technically, I say. Des Moines is a metropolitan city and all, but from where I am, I can stand up and see two unlocked bikes parked in a garage that does not even have a door on it—which, after fifteen years in Chicago, just seems like perversion. Iowa the reality is much like the Iowa of my imagination.

The night is so silent that we cannot even walk around our rental, the creakiest home ever to be offered to overnight guests on the internet, for fear of waking our sleeping children. There is almost a druggy novelty to it, all the silence and safety tipping us out of reality, like too-stoned teenagers exiting their dorm room and finding the mundane world to be "weiiiiird." My husband and I huddle in the kitchen and slowly open a bag of chips. We keep our crunching deliberate.

I have come, a wary visitor. I had never heard my sister so upset and over-the-phone comfort did not feel like enough. So we packed up the children and all their supplies, which include a folding mini-crib, toys for chewing, cars small enough for in-car use, a stuffed dog that has been dressed in a preemie diaper and onesie for the last week, and books for long and short attention spans, and embarked on our six-hour odyssey.

It is always nice to get out of the city, but this trip is not about that. My sister was sobbing because her friend had been shot six times, as had her friend's boyfriend, who had been lying on top of the girl to protect her from the gunman, who happened to be the girl's mother's abusive boyfriend. This man then shot and killed the mother and himself. The mother had been attempting to move out of the home they shared. She was a family friend, had dated my stepdad after he and my mom split up. I was eighteen and out of the house then, out in Los Angeles, and so my memories of her are vague—she was blonde and nice and seemed to be a comfort for our dad. The papers in Minneapolis called it "femicide," which bothers me, as it seems to imply women being killed by their husbands or boyfriends is some new, novel thing—that it needs a separate designation.

We've come to Iowa to be of service. We have two little boys who are valuable as a distraction and so we are here to deploy them like those comfort dogs they bring to colleges during finals week. Children can pull you back from grief. William, very nearly three, has of late been engaging me on the topic of why don't I have a penis, then running down a long list of people/animals/relatives in his life and telling me whether they do or do not have a penis themselves. Sometimes he offers, as if to console me, that "one day" I will grow a penis, a butt, and a beard; that one day I will be a daddy. It is like living with a teeny-tiny Freud, all this talk about a penis it is assumed I wish to own. Meanwhile Jude, the Younger, has a small arsenal of party tricks, impressive given that he is one year old—some rudimentary harmonica skills, the tendency to yell "POW!" when he gives you a high-five. They are too young to know how much they salve us with their very existence.

The drive was fine; even the people in the car who are allowed to shit their pants didn't. I lobbed a few questions at my husband, who went to college here and lived in Iowa City for a time. The Iowa I know is his telling of it—which is mostly oriented around his impossibly gross stories of working in a surgical pathology lab, an unfortunate jazz recital where he sat in with Wynton Marsalis, and his job driving a campus bus. We drive through Iowa City, pit-stop at the co-op, and then drive around until we lay eyes on it. See, William? This is the bus that made your father a man.

Within hours of our arrival in Des Moines my mom comes down with an illness that, in another era, probably would have landed her in an iron lung—charging my sister with the care of our bedridden mother as well as her small menagerie of impossible dogs and a smush-faced kitten who has a problem with life and so never ceases meowing. Which is to say we spend most of our time without either of them, puttering in a funny orbit around Des Moines for a weekend. We eat at my mom's favorite restaurant without her, a Vietnamese spot incredibly named A Dong, which we know of from her many excited and earnest check-ins on Facebook, with their accompanying posts about how much she loves eating A Dong. This is all true, McSweeney's.

The place we stay has no wireless internet—the hostess's explanation being simply: "My son is fifteen." I look at the pictures of this boy around the house and think about the things we do to try to keep boys good. The events that brought us to

Des Moines have me dwelling on that, on all we do in hopes of raising good boys, on living in quiet fear of whatever it is that turns a boy bad.

The boy who lives in that house, this internetless boy, he looks like a good one. He has an agate collection and a Chinese workbook and dinosaur sheets on his bed where my own good boy is asleep.

On the long drive home we talk about Iowa's idyll—we consider it. A little house with a long lawn where the boys could run shoeless and free. While stopped (again) at the co-op in Iowa City, alone in the car with the baby sleeping, a miniature Carnaval-style children's parade passes by me in the rain, trailed by a salsa band crammed onto a flatbed. It feels like a dream; I am the only one who sees it as they cruise past. A moment later, as I start to explain to William what he missed while they were in the store, a mom dressed as a tree walks past and shakes some ginger candies out of her crudely formed treetop hat for him.

I think I've fallen in love with Iowa a bit.

Yours from Paradise,

JESSICA HOPPER
CHICAGO, IL

from ISSUE 39

DEAR MCSWEENEY'S,

I promised I'd be in touch soon after my last letter, but the year blinked past, time evaporated, and so I apologize that "soon" evidently means "more than a year." We're moving, that's one thing. Figuring that out has been taking a lot of time. Believe me, too, it brings out the neighbors, who now pay us all kinds of attention and offer loads of advice about what we should be doing. The driveway needs more gravel, the front railing could use another coat, things like that. We should weed the lawn better, I'm told.

Since my last note, our one neighbor (the trampoline house) lost her battle with cancer. She passed away. We actually didn't even know; we were so used to ambulance sounds that it didn't occur to us for a while that the last visit was just that, the last visit. I was getting the mail when I saw Billy's car drive by with REST IN PEACE and birth and death dates soaped onto the back window.

Half the time I beam with pride at how much I pay attention; that's the key, right? You just have to pay attention to others, acknowledge the humanity of those around you, and society will prosper. So okay, but the other half of the time is this embarrassing ignorance of the world and everyone in it. If pressed, I have to admit I spend a lot more time there on that other half than a healthy self-image can allow. Not to mention that when your neighbors use the attention you do give them to dole out unsolicited advice it makes you question the whole equation.

But the neighbor catty-corner to our backyard? I finally saw him. For the first time in five years I saw him. How's that. They're making a big deal right now out of how the people in Abbottabad didn't know who was living in that high-walled compound, but even though there are any number of questions I might pose to Pakistan, that wouldn't be one of them. I have no idea what the guy across the way has been doing for the last five years, sixty feet from my kids' swing set. I mean, I can't tell if this is his summer home, if he has family, if he has one car or two, if that wire-fenced garden that's somehow growing something is maybe secretly tended to in the middle of the night.

Not long after I spotted him, maybe the next week, my wife, C—, was looking out our back kitchen window trying to get a peek at him herself. Instead she saw Billy with his dogs waddling under our swing set on a long leash, scratching at the dirt, about to crap. She's seen him walking the property line out back for years, not to mention the front walk. I think I mentioned that in my last letter. Depending on her mood, this has caused surprise, irritation, anger, and seething rage. We've had to live here, though, so what can you do?

But this time his dogs were ranging way into our yard, obviously past the property line, not just dancing along it to leave you wondering, Well, I dunno, is that crossing the line, too? This was more blatant. And so, not even thinking, my wife yanked the sliding door open and blurted out, "Oh, come on already with the dogs, Billy! My kids play there!"

His head snapped up, and that gruff smoker's voice said, "Okay, oh, okay, okay." Then he jerked them back to his side.

C— surprised herself, being so brash, and then got embarrassed that it might be disrespectful, given his circumstances. She was out picking weeds a few days later up by the street when Billy drove by on his way home, slowing his car as he approached our drive. REST IN PEACE was long faded off the back window, no doubt washed away by the rain. C— was a little nervous, dirt-covered dandelion leaves in hand, when he stopped. He's a big guy. Like, car-leaning-to-the-side big. But he just propped his arm out the window and said, "You know, I respect you just came right out and told me that. You didn't call the cops on us or nothin', you talked straight to me about it. I want you to know I respect that."

That was all. Then he drove on.

I guess she'd kept the order in our neighborhood. Maybe it was easier for her to do it then; she wasn't worried about paying attention to the universe except to notice what was right in front of her. Maybe she blurted that out because it's not our home anymore, not for much longer. I don't know what I'm supposed to think about it or anything else, really, but I have this hunch that the next time I write, from our new home, in another state, with a new job and new schools and new neighbors, I'll probably romanticize our life back here. It'll all be so beautiful and clear.

Take care, for now,

BENJAMIN COHEN
CHARLOTTESVILLE, VA

DEAR MCSWEENEY'S,

Yesterday I went to get an ultrasound, following up on a mammogram I got a week or so ago. I was pretty cavalier about this, having dense breasts as I do, which is a thing: the women in my family all have dense breasts, and it means that whenever you get a mammogram they can't quite *see* things clearly, like looking through a fogged-up windshield, perhaps, or a frosted one, and so I have to go back and get an ultrasound where you recline with your arms stretched above your head while a stranger squirts warm jelly (it sounds gross, but it's better than cold jelly) all over your breasts and then runs the little ultrasound wand over you, back and forth, back and forth. Medical insurance being what it is in this country (horrid), this means that even though I *know* I have dense breasts and that a regular mammogram will not provide an adequate spy into my breast tissue, I have to go through the charade of the initial, ineffective mammogram and only then can a doctor order an insurance-covered follow-up ultrasound. Am I complaining? Yes and no. I have health insurance, which is amazing. It's sooooo expensive but somehow we afford it—well, not somehow; I know how. My spouse was in the right place at the right time and plus is a hardworking Virgo with a solid middle-class work ethic plus is genderqueer or whatever so had to work super-duper hard to prove that even though they're a freak or whatever they are such an asset to their company, which they are, and now we can afford health insurance, thank you, Dashiell.

Can I interrupt this tale to tell you I'm writing this in a cafe in Los Angeles and the person sitting next to me just name-dropped Jesse Tyler Ferguson, one of the gays from *Modern Family*, on the business call they are on right now? They just hung up with a director they are *really* excited to be working with; they really clicked over an *I Love Lucy* reference. This happens all the time in Los Angeles, of course, and it is so preferable to San Francisco, where everyone really is talking about tech companies all around you at restaurants and cafes, you can't escape it, and even if someone is quiet they're wearing a Google T-shirt or something. I like this better. I actually saw Jesse Tyler Ferguson at Intelligentsia Coffeebar one day, just sitting and talking to a friend outside. My spouse and I once went on a date to this little French restaurant where we were seated right by Jenny Slate, who is my spouse's "hall pass" or whatever, but my spouse was going through this big allergy flare-up and their lips swelled out *so big* while we were sitting there, just huge and crazy like the worst joke of a bad lip job, and I felt bad for them, face-to-face with their celebrity crush, which really hardly ever happens to anyone, even here in LA, and they were having this terrible face issue. But the next time we were there the room was empty save for us and a writer from that show *Mozart in the Jungle*, which I watched only once but couldn't get too into, and the writer talked loudly about their life and it was impossible not to listen, so my spouse and I sat quietly eating our *frites* just listening to this person's life. He name-dropped another TV writer and what is so funny is that on our *next* date we were, at a different restaurant, seated next to *that* TV writer! If I'm making it sound like you can move to Los Angeles and dine around television people all the time, it's because you can, but don't think that that means it's easy to make it in Hollywood or anything, because I am here to tell you that it is not.

So, back at my follow-up ultrasound, I realize that I was called back not because of dense breasts per se but because there was *something* on my initial mammogram. Something that wasn't on the last one. So they needed to do the ultrasound with the warm jelly, and the woman just keeps digging and digging and sliding the wand over this one area and I guess that's where the *something* is. And I start crying. I can't believe it. Thankfully, it's just a few tears and the woman is very intent on the screen she is staring into but now I am thinking that I am going to die and I have a four-year-old and this now makes dying terrible, awful, the worst. And I can't stop thinking about it, I'm flooded with tragic vibes. I *know* that chances are it's actually nothing, and that even if it's something chances are that that something is nothing, and even if the something is something, it's probably benign, and even if it is not benign chances are I will survive, like the breast cancer survivors I know. The chances of this being the beginning of the end are slight, but this knowledge does not prevent me from plunging into weeping. I can't believe we're all going to die and leave behind so many unfinished projects, families, relationships. What about that guy who is suing his parents because he hadn't asked to be born and they had him for their own amusement? I love that guy; he is totally correct. I think about this all the time—that I didn't do my son any favors by birthing him into this world and what if I up and die now? I mean, what about the fact that I am going to die, if not now, eventually? How will it ever be okay?

The woman leaves the room and I wipe the warm jelly out of my armpit and off my breast with my hospital gown. I get dressed and go into the bathroom and weep. I thought it was going to be just a little teeny cry, like when they fill your coffee up too high and you need to slosh some out to add your almond milk. But I'm really crying. It takes longer than I anticipated and I leave with my sunglasses on because my face is so red and puffy. How will I be able to lie to my spouse as planned when I return home with my face all red and puffy? I've decided not to say anything until I get the results in two days. Why freak anyone out? I imagine having a secret cancer diagnosis, like the woman in *My Life Without Me*. I love that movie, though I bet I couldn't watch it now, now that I'm a mom too. I think about recording voice messages for Atti to play for the rest of his motherless life: of course I will have to do that. I don't feel the need to seduce anyone before I die, like she did, having seduced enough people, and anyway, I wouldn't have to have a cancer diagnosis to sleep with Mark Ruffalo, I think Dashiell would be understanding if that opportunity presented itself and I took advantage of it.

At home I just tell Dashiell right away as they're getting into the shower. It's Tuesday, which means our son has a longer day at school and so it's the day we have sex. I mean, we could have sex any day, sort of/not really, but at least on Tuesday we *know* we will have sex, also get brunch, and Dashiell makes it clear that we of course do not have to have sex; we can just lie around in bed together and whatnot but *no*, I am not going to let what is not even a thing get in the way of our sex life, and plus if I am dying then I want to *live* until I die, and that means sex, lots of sex with Dashiell, but when I go into the kitchen to squash up an avocado and eat it with crackers, I can't stop crying, and even as I then eat a piece of toast with almond butter and jam, the sugar-free jam because cancer feeds on sugar, doesn't it, I can't stop crying, so then I return to Dashiell, who is taking a long shower, which means they are probably crying, too, because they pride themselves on their short showers, and I tell them I actually am too fragile to have sex. I mean, who wants to have sex with a crying person. Bummer.

We lie in bed and Dashiell essentially tells me Atti will be fine without me and even having had me as a mom for four years is such a gift. This might sound terrible to you but it is exactly what I want to hear. Dashiell and I cuddle all wound up and pretzeled and it is *so* nice because our kid sleeps between us, which means we never get to cuddle anymore and it feels so good I could fall asleep. I have a sinus cold and the crying has really exacerbated it. I decide I'll take a shower and we'll go out for food. I go into the bathroom and take off my clothes and take my dirty hair out of the bun and brush it all out so it is like a crazy clown wig, like Krusty the Clown from *The Simpsons* exactly, and in that state I return to the bedroom and tell Dashiell that from the way the woman kept running the ultrasound wand over this one part of my breast, I know something is there, she was trying to capture it. After she left the room I looked at the screen and way at the bottom there were little thumbnails of each shot of my breast and I could tell some of them had neon orange spots and I imagined that that was where the computer had detected *cancer*. But I was too afraid to click around. I realize my hair looks so crazy and I'm naked and I quickly summon my dignity and leave.

Dashiell actually forgot they had to work at the preschool this afternoon, can you believe it. I actually can believe it; they are sort of forgetful. Maybe it's the vitamin B deficiency or else that they sleep terribly every night, or adolescent weed-smoking or a traumatic childhood, we're not sure. I feel so bad that they have to go to work at the school feeling *freaked out*, which they acknowledge they are feeling. When I climb out of the shower they are gone.

I go to the cafe where everyone is working on their screenplays and I get a bagel and cream cheese and a coffee and read Alexander Chee's *How to Write an Autobiographical Novel.* I walk to the thrift store down the street, texting my friend and my sister and my AA sponsee about my mammogram problem. My sister calls me right away. She is a hypochondriac and great in situations of other people's potential medical issues. She goes on Komen.org and assures me it's likely nothing and that breast cancer, unlike dense breasts, does not run in our family. And I breastfed. She feels too bad for me to let me off the phone but I eventually need the soothing environment of the thrift store, which is run by a sect of young Christians who are very sweet even though I always want to hold a grudge against a Christian, for the obvious reasons. I buy an interesting gold necklace and a pair of enamel earrings and for my son I find a Captain America shield that doubles as a *purse*, if you can believe it, then buy five kids' books so I can get the 50 percent–off discount: *Pinocchio* (Disney version), an Eric Carle book about a hermit crab, a lift-the-flap 1980s book about the human body, a story about an elephant who goes to Venice, Italy, because we are going to Venice, Italy, in May, and then a book about a little bunny that won't stop saying, "Poop-di-doop!," which I think my son will love because he himself cannot stop saying "poop" and "poopoohead" and "kill" and "die" and "dead" and "hate" and "pee."

At the preschool my spouse looks so weary running around cleaning everything up and I watch my son go down the slide a bunch, each time landing on his feet in a sort of pose, and I heap much praise upon him, though his friend Maisie actually lands on her feet and seamlessly transitions into a somersault and that is the real winner. In the car I sit in the backseat with him and read the elephant book, which is sort of weird and boring and keeps talking about how great Diet Coke is, and then the poop-di-doop book, which, as I guessed, he loves. They drop me off at the cafe because I still have to work, the submission to that HBO script workshop is still due today, my e-mails are still languishing in my inbox, and so I go inside and set up my computer and get my new thing, a double espresso and a huge bottle of Topo Chico: it's caffeinating and also refreshing. And while I am working my phone rings and it's a Los Angeles number so I pick up in case it's my manager, and it's Betty from my doctor's office. Dashiell loves Betty. Dashiell has that vibe where they can charm older ladies and through the injecting of many vitamin B shots they have come to love each other, and Betty tells me my ultrasound is normal. I didn't expect to hear anything today. I run out of the cafe with my phone even though everyone is always loudly making deals on theirs in this cafe, I run out and stop myself from telling Betty all about my day. I text Dashiell and I text my sister and my friend and my AA sponsee. I feel so good and we all go out and eat Mexican food for dinner and after dinner, when our son is asleep, I make a small batch of really weird cookies. I thought we were out of chocolate chips so I put in cocoa and cinnamon and then Dashiell found the chips and I put all of them in, too many, and it was Earth Balance instead of butter and maybe the recipe was bad, the sugar-to-flour ratio was off, but we eat them anyway and guzzle milk and watch *The Chilling Adventures of Sabrina* and Dashiell lies down because their back hurts and I put a pillow on their butt and put my head there and they sort of pet my head while I sort of pet the cat so he doesn't get jealous. And we watch TV and then we go to sleep.

Thankfully,

MICHELLE TEA
LOS ANGELES, CA

MCSWEENEY'S CUSTOMER SERVICE,

I just purchased an eighty-gram bag of McSweeney's Turkey Jerky from a gas station in Lacombe, Alberta, and it doesn't taste very good. Unfortunately, I'm not happy with the product. I've purchased the Turkey Jerky multiple times before at other convenience stores and it looked and tasted great! I also noticed that the color of the jerky in this bag looks yellow compared to the other ones I've had, which were pink.

CHUCK HEFFERNAN
LACOMBE, AB

HEY CHUCK,

I'm afraid you've caught the wrong McSweeney's: we're the book publisher, not the jerky maker. I can assure you our books taste even worse than you claim their jerky tastes.

Yours,

MCSWEENEY'S CUSTOMER SUPPORT
SAN FRANCISCO, CA

DEAR MCSWEENEY'S,

The older I get, the more I realize how the breadth and depth of most human conversation is very limited. I mean, I meet my friends at coffee joints like everyone else, and we have the usual parley—"I can't go on; I'll go on," etc.—but there really isn't room in most daily interchanges for the important topics, the meaningful ones, that make life worth living.

You know something I think about that I can't say to my friends over coffee? I can't say, You know, I'm not sure I believe in the power of the written word anymore. I can't say, Look, there is only one good book that has ever been written and it's a hundred and fifty years old and its name is *Walden*. Do you know how good *Walden* is? It's so good that we should eat it. It's so good that it should be ground up and sprinkled on our food. It is so good that every letters-to-the-editor page in every printed-on-paper newspaper around the world should be replaced with quotes from *Walden*:

> A slight sound at evening lifts me up by the ears,
> and makes life seem inexpressibly serene and

grand. It may be in Uranus, or it may be in the
shutter.

That is so good it is insane. Here's what I think: I think we
are coming into a new era, an era in which the written word
won't matter much anymore. What will matter in the future is
not what we say with words, or what we write with words, but
what we *do* with words. And I have an idea about that: I think
words should go on toast. I think one word in particular should
go on toast, and then we should eat that word/toast every day
and say that word all day long.

The word I have in mind is *peace*, but I don't know how to
get that on my toast, so I am experimenting now, like Thoreau,
with what I have at hand, with what is around me, with what
is available. I have gone to my high-speed internet connection,
which has in turn directed me to the NFL online gift shop.

Now this is what you do, to create a peace-toast word-world,
for yourself, in your home. First, go online to the NFL gift shop
and purchase two toasters, each of which will emblazon your
toast with the emblem of an NFL team. You must buy toasters
with the emblems of two rival teams. If you pick two teams
that never play each other, the experiment won't work. I myself
have purchased one toaster for the New York Giants, and one
for the New York Jets.

Each child in my house, each morning, sits down to a Jets-
Giants Nutella-toast sandwich. I have three kids; that means at
least six pieces of toast each morning. Sometimes ten.

I stand over them while they eat. Taste the chocolatey,
hazelnut goodness, I say. Taste the sweetness between bitter
Eastern Division opponents. Taste the flavor of the pieces/peaces
of wheat bread that are also a book that also offers you chocolate, a book that is food, which is words, which are right

now connecting you and other people on Earth in a fabulous, sticky, and slightly incomprehensible way. Savor the ineffable, *Walden*-esque, chocolate-toast bookword, here at this Sharpie-scarred dining table in New York City, and know, as you wipe the crumbs off your mouth, your simultaneously big and small place in the task of transforming this strange world.

Then I say, Now go and get ready for school.

AMY FUSSELMAN
NEW YORK, NY

from ISSUE 35

DEAR MCSWEENEY'S,

San Francisco, New Orleans, New York, Baltimore, Boston, and Los Angeles: what do these cities have in common? If you guessed "They have all been mentioned in songs by the Counting Crows," you would be correct. If you guessed "All have previously been host to a *McSweeney's*-related event," you would be correct again, and closer to the point.

With your background in systematic logic, I'm sure you have by now divined the thesis of my letter: none of the aforementioned cities is Temecula, California.

As a resident of Temecula, reader of *McSweeney's*, and supporter of public displays of literacy, I have long desired to attend one of the many events that I see advertised on your website. Sadly, distance and the rising cost of bus travel have thus far prevented me from doing so. Other factors contributing to my absence from every *McSweeney's* event ever held include: a temporary injunction against leaving the state of New Mexico, a fear of odd-numbered interstates, and conflicting Lilith Fair tour dates.

I'm sure at this point you're thinking something like, Wait. Isn't Temecula only one hour and thirty-two minutes from Los

Angeles (up to two hours and fifty minutes with traffic)? And isn't Los Angeles a frequent host to *McSweeney's*-sponsored readings, release parties, and various other events ending in -*fest* or -*palooza*?

While you're technically correct, what you have perhaps failed to notice is that the prescribed route to Los Angeles traverses Chino Hills State Park. What's wrong with Chino Hills State Park, you ask? Chino Hills State Park is cougar country. And I don't trust my car or my legs enough to risk a trip through cougar country.

Look: we could spend all afternoon brainstorming creative ways to get me to a *McSweeney's* event without forcing me to miss work or aggravating my peanut allergy, but why bother? I have already come up with a solution that is both convenient and tax-deductible (for me, I mean): you should come to Temecula.

If you're like most people, you probably don't know much about Temecula beyond its nickname, "The city where the 2009 comedy *The Goods*, starring Jeremy Piven, was set." While we are proud of our cinematic heritage, it is but one aspect of who we are as a city.

For example, did you know that Temecula (incorporated 1989) is one of the two California cities to retain its original Indian name? Did you know that Beverly Hills is the other? My guess is you did not. Temecula has a way of surprising you like that.

Plus, since Temecula is only a few years older than *McSweeney's*, I bet you guys are into a lot of the same activities and actresses and stuff. Like, for example, do you love Maggie Gyllenhaal and commuting to San Diego for work? No way! Us too!

In addition to shared interests, there are many locations in Temecula which are ideally suited for a *McSweeney's* event. What we lack in independent bookstores and student centers at liberal arts colleges, we make up for in wineries (more than thirty!), Coffee Beans (three), and foreclosed homes (several thousand). These venues become problematic if you're expecting more than a dozen attendees, but that's okay. The nearby Pechanga Resort and Casino has a showroom with seating for twelve hundred, not to mention some of the loosest slots in the state and a better-than-decent lobster dinner.

If it's a more rustic evening you're after, you could rent out one of the antique boutiques or beer gardens in Temecula's historic Old Town district. And should you arrive early, whether to prep the menu or as part of the advance security detail, you must make time to visit a few of my favorite Old Town shoppes [sic], like The Back Porch, The Farmer's Wife, and Jack's Nuts. These delightful stores are guaranteed to satisfy any and all of your cravings for hand-carved furniture, kitchenware, and nuts, respectively.

Temecula may not have the name recognition or season of *The Real World* to compete with your traditional host cities, but there is much about "The Milwaukee of Riverside County" that you will fall in love with. Jazz festivals, hot-air balloons, and Splash Canyon Waterpark (opening summer 2010) are a few examples.

Am I saying the *McSweeney's* book signing, singles mixer, or three-on-three basketball tournament held in Temecula will be the best one ever? Not necessarily. But I am saying if we advertise in the *North County Times* and get a decent hype man, there is a chance that former Denver Broncos running back and current Temecula resident Terrell Davis will attend.

All I'm saying is, think about it.

Sincerely,

KENT WOODYARD
TEMECULA, CA

from ISSUE 8

DEAR KEVIN,

You know how the nightstands of hotel rooms always have those little copies of the Bible? From time to time I think about publishing a little book of stories and having my father leave them behind in the hotel rooms, just tucked inside the nightstand, right next to the Bible. My father used to travel quite a bit, staying in his share of hotel rooms. I'd have to maintain a map of the world, inserting colored pushpins into the places where my father left the book of stories. Then I'd wait to hear from people. Of course, I always figure on hearing from people. Like you, I like the idea of someone coming across the writing completely by accident, of someone being just exhausted and opening the nightstand expecting exactly what they always expect: a room service menu, maybe a notepad, a couple of complimentary pens, some promotional postcards, and that old Bible. But this time it's a bit different. This time, there's this other book in addition to the expected book.

But what does it mean that we favor the surprised reaction of the unaware person to one who is more knowing?

EDITOR

DEAR EDITOR,

Honesty, maybe. Do you ever wonder how honest your own opinions about literature are? I mean, we read books in school and assume we should be reading them because a teacher swears they have value. We read books as adults and assume we should be reading them because the reviews were all so good, or some editor pre-approved them for us. A story found by accident, however, a story of unknown provenance, is a rare thing.

KEVIN GUILFOILE
CHICAGO, IL

HELLO, MCSWEENEY'S!

At the University of Chicago Press website, I found a list of poems from an anthology titled *Surrealist Love Poems*. At first, I thought I was reading short poems. Then I realized I was reading a list of poem titles. Found poetry, no?

> Andre Breton
> Free union
> I dream I see your image
> Always for the first time
> They tell me that over there
> As they move
> In the lovely twilight
> On the road to San Romano
>
> Robert Desnos
> I have so often dreamed of you
> No, love is not dead
> If you knew
> Sleep spaces

Oh pangs of love!
Never anyone but you
The voice of Robert Desnos
Obsession

Paul Eluard
Your mouth with golden lips
The shape of your eyes
I love you
The earth is blue like an orange
I've told you
As you rise
The lover
About one, two, everyone
Since it must be
Our life

Joyce Mansour
Your breath in my mouth
You love to lie in our unmade bed
I want to show myself naked
Remember
The storm sketches a silver margin
I want to sleep with you

Benjamin Péret
Wink
Hello
Do you know
Fountain

Thanks to all at McSweeney's for the work you do.

GREG CHAPMAN

DEAR MCSWEENEY'S,

The *Twilight* books have ruined my life. They've cast a light onto my own sad existence; not a soft, comforting twilight, but a bright yellow fluorescent light that illuminates my blemishes. Before, I was happy to kiss boys because they were funny, clever, or didn't spit when they spoke. Now my standards have changed.

My friends just think it's funny. They keep teasing me for fancying the anemic boy from school: "*Ooh*, Elizabeth, here's a bright red apple, why don't you take it to Charlie and talk to him about forbidden love? I think he's in the nurses' office because he didn't have any protein at lunch." I know it's a teenage cliché to say "Nobody understands me," but seriously, nobody understands me.

Like Bella, the female protagonist of the *Twilight* books, I moved to a new town last year, and just like Forks, where Bella lives, it's really rainy. (Although, to be honest, most towns in England are rainy.) But this place has rain that's heavy and leaves the air moist and thick; rain that feels ominous and fantastical, you know? I also live with my dad, like Bella, although he isn't a surly police officer. He works in advertising. And the idea that

I would have to cook him dinner each night because he can't look after himself is laughable. That's what he's marrying Carol for.

Recently, anyway, this boy called Simon asked me to the cinema. He's nice and always has gum, but what's the point? His mum's definitely not beautiful enough to be immortal. She wears saggy beige Ugg boots and gets her hair dyed ginger by a man who calls himself Giorgio but definitely isn't Italian. I guess maybe if Simon got a tan he might look like Jacob Black, the werewolf, but Jacob Black always has his shirt off and Simon has to wear a vest in PE because of his pigeon chest.

When I say this stuff to my friends, they joke that I need therapy. Do you think I need therapy? What would I say to a therapist? "I'm depressed that when a boy I like walks into the sunlight, his skin isn't going to sparkle"?

I was thinking about all this on Wednesday, when I cut my hand. Not on purpose; I was cutting a carrot for dinner—I'm on this sort of intense diet—and my finger started bleeding. I remembered this thing my gran had said about how your own saliva is the best way to clot blood, so I put my finger in my mouth. And suddenly, there it was. The taste.

It was warm and salty, just like Stephenie Meyer said it would be in the books. I know it's silly, but I found it kind of exciting.

After about five minutes, the blood stopped coming, and I didn't think of it again until a few days ago. I was in the house on my own and I just started *craving* that taste again. I know I'm not a vampire, because you can't turn yourself into one just by tasting your own blood, otherwise everyone who ever cut themselves would now be a vampire, which they're not. But maybe it doesn't happen like that? Maybe the vampire urge was always in me, inert and waiting for the right moment to erupt? Like racism?

Yesterday I googled "real-life vampire" and found this woman who says her name is Redangel. She lives in Cornwall, and she says she has a contact at a hospital who gets her all her blood. "It's not ideal, but at least I know it's clean," she writes. She says she's not sensitive to light, the way some vampires are, but she's definitely "more of a night owl." She wants me to visit her and her friends over the summer, but I'm not sure I should. Carol would totally freak out.

Maybe it's my parents' fault for splitting up when I was young. That and the fact that they took me to Disney World repeatedly when I was a child and highly impressionable. It's completely ruined real life for me. I look out the window at my stupid street in my stupid town in this stupid country and I think, There must be something more. The idea of spending the rest of my days with nothing fantastical ever happening makes me so depressed I sometimes stay in bed for a whole day. Carol says it's just growing pains, and rubs my back in a way that she probably thinks is comforting and maternal. But it's not, it's just creepy.

ELIZABETH SANKEY
LONDON, ENGLAND

DEAR MCSWEENEY'S,

A few years ago, in my early twenties, my daddy's ghost started appearing to me, and I found myself in a psych ward at Mercy Hospital. I'd been in Iowa City only three months, at first smothered by the humidity of summer, then elated by the splendor of autumn, and then chilled by the raw winter. It was the last week of November, and a fucking apocalypse had taken hold of the place. They called it the coldest winter in twenty years, so that even the Iowa veterans shambled across the ice-slicked streets, shivering in their puffy coats, eyes watery above cold-slapped cheeks. Seeing that others were suffering as I was gave me some comfort—a whole lot of comfort, in fact. We were cuddled in a communal victimhood at the hands of some enraged weather god, the combined efforts of Khione, Greek goddess of snow, and Shango, Yoruba god of thunder, et cetera, who together were taking pleasure in this damn shit visited upon us, this fucking crazy winter with the clouds pimpled and surly like the tumult of adolescence. The sun was coldhearted even on the brightest of days. Not one ray of love.

I think this was when my body or my mind, or a tag team of body and mind, decided that it was having none of this craziness, and my daddy's ghost decided to make an appearance. I'd already been having some out-of-body experiences, ever since I'd landed at the Cedar Rapids airport in the unbelievable heat of late August and found none of the glitz of LaGuardia, none of that glamour they stuff down our developing-world throats on TV, advertising, selling, outright flaunting that American dream we can all attain if only we try hard enough. That collective vision of us all singing "Kumbaya" in a diamond-studded limousine in a Beyoncé video. Finding none of this, my feet tried to turn away from the BAGGAGE CLAIM sign back toward the NO ENTRY area, begging to step back onto a plane and return to some proper normalcy, *please.*

But there was still some solace to be found even then. Seated in the back of the yellow cab on the drive from the airport, careening down the I-380, the sprawling maize fields—*cornfields*—of Iowa were an instant point of intimacy. Gazing at those sun-washed, shimmering rows of stalks, their reedy bodies sashaying to some tranquil wind-sonata, I was immediately at one with the land and the people of America. For I might as well have been in our own fields back home in Richmond, Bulawayo, Zimbabwe, where I grew up. Mesmerized by this corny déjà vu, I was attacked by that violent bitch nostalgia; my feet began to itch, my hands began to tremble, and I swear a rabid watering overtook my mouth. It took all of me not to implore the driver to stop so I could swing open the taxi door, shimmy my plump behind off the hot leather seat, and make a dash for those fields. I could see myself frolicking among the blond-bearded husks, summoning my childhood through the feel of the soil, moist and crumbly beneath my feet.

I left a piece of my heart out there in those maize fields on that first day in this serene little piece of America. During those months leading to my sojourn at Mercy Hospital, I deliberately asked cabs to drive past those viridian stalks, just so I could feast my eyes on a marigold kernel peeping from a trembling leaf and witness the silky tassels blowing in the breeze. This habit was, at least for a time, able to fill the hole created by my diminishing sense of self.

With the benefit of hindsight, I realize it was no coincidence that of all the places I could have landed in America—land of cream, honey, Coke, Whataburgers, McFries, (sweetened) corn flakes, (sweetened) cheese, (sweetened) water, and, would you believe it, (sweetened) pills—I had gotten a scholarship to do an MFA program in creative writing at the Iowa Writers' Workshop, Iowa City, Nowhere America. (*Creative writing*, of all the sensible degrees a forward-thinking, historically disenfranchised Person of Color from the Developing World could have chosen to attain.) I believe strongly—no, *I know*—that it was my daddy's ghost that led me to the quiet, out-of-the-way, corny Midwest. Because my daddy had been trying to communicate with me for a long time, and I'd been running, outright fleeing, because isn't it the most terrifying thing to have your daddy's ghost appearing to you?

I had some valid excuses for not being able to hear him, though. I'd been deep in the noise. Back home in Bulawayo, the noise was screaming-pitch high, and I was lost in it, drowning in it, probably screaming also; too numb, tired, worried, or doing some plain-desperate shit like biting hands and elbowing ribs in some never-ending bread queue or mealie-meal queue or cooking-oil queue, and, during my last months home, before undergrad in Johannesburg, the longest damn visa queue I've ever been in.

The noise, once I got to Johannesburg, was just as screaming-pitch high; big cities are by nature made for distraction. I understand now that whatever calamities I've faced in my life have been because it's been too loud in my head, and I haven't been able to hear my ancestors, or Jesus, or is it my ancestors *and* Jesus, meshing into a woke cosmopolitan spirit guide who is a mix of ancestral mystery and Christian myth, because damned if I know how this post-postcolonial identity mess gets resolved. Like, you can't wallow in a mythical past forever, and you sort of can't deny the path of violence that has formed you, but you also have to transcend that (post)colonial shit and all that trauma that history has heaped upon your back. And maybe you do that through the guiding spirituality of a dialectical, avant-garde twenty-first-century ancestral Jesus, who, in line with the times, has rediscovered his radicalness and written a post-postmodern novel named *Bible Reborn*.

And so, in the freakishly tranquil Iowa City, where I could walk around at any time of day or night, ambling past unfenced homes and family cars parked on the street, I had no choice but to sit with this damn silence and finally hear my daddy's ghost calling out to me. Such stillness in a place so white and so foreign catapults you into some sober reflection. Having lost a sense of who you are, you begin to scramble desperately in search of yourself. No one in Iowa City could pronounce my name. Everyone tripped over the syllables. It's a beautiful name, one of the easiest names to pronounce in my Ndebele language. So I began to go by my second name, Rosa. The constant sound of it in the mouths of others made me feel like a different person, a thrilling transgression, like I was putting on an identity. My flatmate, Shaniqua, who was also at the Iowa Writers' Workshop, said I should insist that these white people call me by my proper name. That's how she said it, "Tell 'em white folk to stop trippin'," her pretty lips lifting at one corner of her mouth. But I told her I did not mind; both my names had been given to me by my father, and for this reason I loved them equally. She looked unimpressed. So I told her my father had named me after Rosa Luxemburg, the Marxist, who had been a revolutionary woman, and that made it a revolutionary name.

The truth was that I had grown embarrassed of myself, ever since arriving in Iowa City. Everywhere I went, people claimed they couldn't hear what I was saying. This hurt. My English was mellifluous; I had attended Girls' College, a private high school back home, where we had etiquette lessons every Monday afternoon our first year, learning to pipe British English through our noses. During those first months in Iowa, I dreaded opening my mouth. When I did, I spoke very slowly, trying my best to enunciate each syllable.

And so you can imagine how happy I was when my daddy started appearing to me, straight from the grave. Shaniqua said I kept talking to myself, and she got scared, and so she called a friend, who called a friend, who called a friend, who'd had a friend just like me from "Africa" who'd been possessed by them "voodoo spirits 'n' shit." After a while, they decided to take me and my voodoo-possessed ass down to Mercy.

Barricaded from the cold by the wide floor-to-ceiling windows on the second floor of the hospital, I thought the snow now looked harmless, falling in a white, delicious fluff, like something that could melt on your tongue. I was charmed by the world before me. Everything was covered by snow, the unfenced single- and double-story houses lined up along East Bloomington Street, the hulking cars parked next to the sidewalks. At night, their laden roofs seemed to emit a phantasmagorical fluorescence, beacons in the pale darkness.

Shaniqua came to see me almost every day. She went on and on about the Iowa Writers' Workshop, or the Workshop, as she called it; who had thrown shade at whom, who had slighted whose work, who had loved whose writing... She wouldn't stop talking about it, and sometimes I wondered why she had come, if she even cared that it was me she was talking to. She never asked about me, or my life, or how my voodoo possession was going, or anything. She'd just sit next to me at one of the round plastic tables in the lounge area of the psych ward during visiting hours, her hands rising every now and then to pat her majestic Afro, going on and on about her life. I sat there meekly listening to her, aware of my situation and grateful for her presence. I tried to grunt politely, laugh where I thought I should, and commiserate with her over one slight or another she had endured during a workshop at the Workshop. I loved her for this, for being there at the psych ward. For showing me such kindness. I did not have anyone.

She even stayed with me after I was released from Mercy, two weeks later, and helped me find my therapist, M, the one person who didn't judge my daddy for being a ghost or me for loving him still, so much so that I never wanted him to leave, even though I knew he'd have to, if I was going to have a chance at this life.

Best,

NOVUYO ROSA TSHUMA
HOUSTON, TX

from ISSUE 3

DEAR MCSWEENEY'S,
Last night, at a bar on Roosevelt Island, an older man called me "Crying Game."

JASON ADAMS
NEW YORK, NY

from ISSUE 11

DEAR MCSWEENEY'S,

Something as small as a four-year-old's speech impediment couldn't have tripped up Rabs. Not even Tammy could.

Tammy was our friend and we loved her. The whole town did. Growing up, you could go into almost any public bathroom, and scratched in some pocked wood, between a bunch of dick-suckers and sluts, you'd see how we all thought: "Tammy is the sweetest."

It's funny, McSweeney's, but even as an avid reader of bathroom walls, this never struck me as strange. Whenever I read something about how smart or funny Tammy was, I'd think of college applications, not obituaries.

We found out about Tammy over the school's PA system. Until then, the biggest thing that ever happened in our town was Friday night. So when we first heard, all we knew to do was get in our cars and drive Main Street. All we knew to say was beep our horns.

Later that night, we met up in my basement. There must have been twenty of us. We were all drinking and crying, and then we started taking turns saying something nice about Tammy. It was just like TV. Our friend Brad, his giant shoulders shaking with grief, told how Tammy would buy him a Big Mac when he was broke. And Lisa, one of those bathroom-wall sluts, said that Tammy always helped her when she got behind in Algebra II. Even I talked about how Tammy was my only friend in fourth grade, the year I wouldn't go outside at recess. Then Rabs spoke, two people ahead of his turn.

"I bet when birds kill themselves, they fall up," he said. "I bet they keep going up and up into the cold sky until their heart beats so fast it shatters inside their tiny bird chest. Their suicides are rare but spectacular."

By then, everyone was pretty much used to Rabs, so they ignored him and went on with their show. But, McSweeney's, looking over at him, sitting on the floor with eyes closed and half a smile, I had to think about Tammy to keep from crying. Rabs was that beautiful.

Sincerely,

TREVOR KOSKI
CHICAGO, IL

DEAR MCSWEENEY'S,

Here's something stupid: my best friend and I didn't speak for three weeks. Is three weeks a long time to go without talking to someone? I'm not sure what the normal amount of time to go without any kind of communication with a friend is, but Baby Braga and I rarely go more than a day. (Baby Braga is, of course, not his Christian name but rather a terrible nickname I gave him when we met, nearly a decade ago, in our first year of university. He hates it, his girlfriend thinks it's idiotic, and his mom is mad that I keep using it in published work, thereby solidifying him in the world as an adult infant. They're all right. I should stop. But I don't experience a lot of natural joy in my life, so I'm clinging to this, a rude name I gave to my friend because at the time he had the head and body of a big baby.)

The point is, Baby Braga and I don't go more than a hot minute without speaking, so three weeks is a lifetime. Whenever I run into people, they ask me about him, as if we were not just good friends who hang out periodically but rather very close siblings. It would be reasonable to ask, *How's your brother doing?* but maybe less reasonable to respond to that question with *I don't fucking know, Adrian, why don't you ask him yourself*, before bursting into tears.

The fight was stupid. I don't know exactly when it started but we'd been trying to plan a group trip together for a few months, and the stress of it all had made us resent each other. The trip was my bachelorette party of sorts, but the term *bachelorette party* makes me want to cover my body in salt and shrink up and die. Planning a trip is one thing, but planning a *bachelorette party* takes on this ugly tone. It stops being a fun thing you do with your friends and becomes an imposition, unforgivable if you don't participate and devastating if organized poorly. Everyone has to express appropriate enthusiasm and celebrate you for, I don't know, finally finding someone who will tolerate you? I just wanted to get very drunk with my terrible friends, but as my maid of honor, Baby Braga likely felt more pressure than I realized.

The strange, never-articulated silence might have started because of the trip, but I suspect the seeds were planted even before that, when I told him that I'm moving later this year. The flight between us will be only an hour and a half, but I'm leaving the country, meaning the journey now feels like an unwanted adventure instead of an easy jaunt. We've lived in the same city since we started university and quickly became inseparable. We don't really have a lot in common (he is a technology reporter and I am still putting tape over my webcam), but what we do have in common has kept us together for longer than any other relationship I've ever had. We hate all the same things (playing board games at bars), all the same places (restaurants with communal seating), all the same people (anyone who Instagrams photos of smoothies). We both really like soup.

So the weight of my move has felt heavy, I guess, for both of us. We met when we were seventeen—the perfect age to make a new friend—and neither of us is particularly interested in new people. Baby Braga has been dating his girlfriend for nearly five years, and at this point they're so melded that they communicate with each other largely through smiles (gross) and furtive glances. I've been with my partner for nearly seven years, and he spoils me with his decency. We've both been set for a long time, no need to go looking for new people to make our lives feel rich. Having to think about making new friends in our late twenties feels like a real goddamn imposition.

I don't think we were really icing each other out because of anything particular, the trip or the move. I think we were both just feeling sad, and we've never had a language for sadness. Baby Braga talks in puns and inane television references (I can't get him to stop talking about *Frasier*), and I talk back in insults and disinterested groans. How do you tell someone whom you love very much—in this particular fashion where they're not the *only* person you love, but rather where they're a deeply important nonromantic person who gives you joy and comfort, whose minutiae you love to hear about ("I got a new hat for next winter" or "I just started making sourdough bread"), whom you need to stay connected and involved with, but not so involved the way a wife or a pet would be involved (sleeping in the same bed, considering each other when you go shopping for a new armchair)—that you're going to miss them so much if they somehow disappear, and how terrifying, though inevitable, change is, because it might affect the nucleus you've worked so hard to maintain all these years, and that thinking about it for too long brings you to spontaneous tears so that the waitress at Jack Astor's comps your three wines, each of which you Jack'd Up to a ten-ounce chalice, just so she can get you out of her section?

I do not know how to say that. But Baby Braga sent me a note after it went on for too long, and we fought briefly over

Facebook Messenger, and then it subsided, and then we decided to have lunch at a Middle Eastern restaurant. I didn't want to order a meal but rather just a bunch of dips and bread, and so when he said, "Do you just want to order a bunch of dips and bread?" without my having to suggest it, I felt my heart swell like I was being seen after a lifetime of being invisible. We ordered four dips (too many) and a giant cauliflower monstrosity covered in pine nuts and pomegranate seeds and tahini, and I wondered how I could ever find another friend who understood me in this particular way, that I want dips and bread and nothing else, that of *course* I don't want to talk about the fight, and that, yes, I just want to pretend as if nothing has changed and nothing will ever change.

When we met for lunch, Baby Braga hugged me and said, "Do you hear that?" and I said, "No, what?" and he said, "That's the sound of friendship." It was the dumbest fucking thing I have ever heard.

Anyway. Talk to you later,

SCAACHI KOUL
TORONTO, ON

DEAR MCSWEENEY'S,

Having been whipped—many times in the nipple—onstage for a paying audience, I have never understood how people could claim to derive sexual pleasure from this sort of activity.

It was November 1994, and I was playing Jesus in *Jesus Christ Superstar* at the University of Virginia. I loved the role, and—well, I won't write my own reviews—but once, passing by a giant snowball fight months after the show, a student I didn't know yelled, "Look, it's Jesus! CRUCIFY HIM!!!" And they did. Scores of them, with a barrage of snowballs. I took that experience positively, if painfully: after all, when you can get the crowds to adore and remember you and then turn on you, you've nailed "Jesus" as an actor.

Still, it's not the snowballs that I remember most; it's the whipping scene. It comes in Act II, "Trial Before Pilate (Including the 39 Lashes)," wherein Jesus is whipped thirty-nine times—or so you, the paying audience, would assume. Actually, he's whipped thirty-nine times for each of the four performances, plus thirty-nine times for each of three full-dress rehearsals, plus as many times as it takes for a few eighteen-year-olds to work out the fake-blood situation. So hundreds upon hundreds of times, really.

The technical team of two women and I worked for hours perfecting the blood mixture, as well as the technique of me not screaming in pain. What we discovered in the process was that in order for our fake-blood combination of water, Karo sauce, and actual human tears to look and act like real blood (so as not to look like Jesus was leaking Kool-Aid), we needed to make it thick. I mean, *thick* thick. Molasses thick. Charlottesville in August thick.

The problem—well, for Jesus, the problem—was that the thicker the fake blood, the more it stuck to human skin. The whipping was painful enough, but a whip that sticks to your skin takes a piece of Jesus as a souvenir with every lash. Worse, the guy playing the Roman guard who whips Jesus never missed. He didn't know his own strength, either. Every night before curtain, I would say to him, "Please, go light. You're whipping me much harder than you think."

"Got it," he'd say.

Then every night the first blow would come light, and the next thirty-eight at full imperial strength.

He and everyone else agreed: it just didn't look real otherwise. Not that they were telling me to take one for Team Jesus; they just assumed the marks on my body were fake, and out of some noble loyalty to the show's aesthetics, I didn't tell anyone that, actually, every night audiences were paying to see a man flayed onstage.

What can I say? The technical team did its job and did it well. The fake blood looked just like the real stuff.

It was Jesus' nipples that suffered the most, though. You see, the blood needed to flow from a high-enough point on the Messiah's back for the audience to see it. That meant aiming as best you could for the upper torso—and that our Roman friend did with great skill. Unfortunately, every fifth or so blow would snake around front and strike Jesus square on his right nipple. The whip was long enough to occasionally hit the left one, as well.

I don't know if you've ever been bullwhipped in the nipple, say, eight times a night for seven nights in a row, but it's not the fun your secret stash of movies makes it out to be. The pain comes in three stages. There's the initial strike, when it lands, at which point no matter how much you've prepared yourself for it, you still lose your breath. Then—at least in this Jesus' case—there's the pain of the whip making that sticky tearing sound as it's ripped away. One time when that happened—a full shot to the right nipple—I nearly fainted.

But it's that moment in between, when the whip has landed and you have a split second to recover from the pain while letting yourself be mentally terrorized by the tearing to come, that really brings you closer to the role. Honestly, between the bits of blood and body I gave, I'm one of the few people who can tell you what it's like to *be* Holy Communion, not just take it.

Had my first association with whips and nipple torture not been so ecclesiastical, perhaps I might hold a different opinion on their sexual allure. But I doubt it.

Yours,

JOHN FLOWERS
BROOKLYN, NY

DEAR MCSWEENEY'S,

I hear there're a lot of Brazilian steakhouses in the States now: waiters dressed as gaúchos with red scarves, cowboy hats, and those baggy pants called *bombachas*; astonishing amounts of hissing meat being carried around on steel skewers; tableside service of said meat directly onto the diner's plate. There's usually an emphasis on what I believe they call "Brazilian sirloin," or *picanha*, a small, triangle-shaped muscle with a thick fat layer. Cows apparently never flex their *picanhas* while they move around at pasture, chewing on grass, so that particular cut stays wonderfully tender and juicy.

I know a bit about all this because so-called Brazilian steakhouses come from Rio Grande do Sul, Brazil's southernmost state, where I live. Fogo de Chão, which has branches in fifteen American cities, appeared here in Porto Alegre in 1979. I used to go there with my family when I was little; they always had huge cow ribcages roasting over the firepits right by the entrance.

What they did was refine and standardize the Porto Alegre steakhouse system we call *espeto corrido*. *Espeto* is the spike on which the meat is impaled and slowly roasted; *corrido* is the participle of *correr*, which means "to run." So there you have it: waiters running around with meat on spikes.

What I'm not so sure about is whether they serve chicken hearts up there in the States, too. One thing I can tell you about Porto Alegre is that we eat a lot of chicken hearts.

Every *espeto corrido*–style *churrascaria* here has dozens of spikes full of roasted chicken hearts being *corrido*'d around at any given time. One of our most beloved local delicacies is the infamous *X-Coração*; it's a sandwich, kind of, and it demands explanation. The letter *X*, in Portuguese, sounds the same as the English word *cheese*, so the *X* stands for "cheese." *Coração* means "heart," which down here is usually going to refer to a chicken heart. So we're talking about a sort of cheeseburger with chicken hearts in place of the hamburger. Except it's also huge, the size of a tambourine.

The X-Coração is pressed, or squashed, really, on a special rectangular hot plate. It tends to include plenty of other ingredients, such as lettuce, tomato, slices of ham, mayonnaise, a whole fried egg, corn, bacon, grilled onions, and string beans. The result is aesthetically unpleasant and structurally weak—the sandwich will fall apart as soon as you start working on it—but it's also delicious. I've treated many outsiders to an X-Coração, and they've all loved it, unless they had some serious issue with chicken hearts or were not especially open to new gourmet experiences.

Our fondness for chicken hearts brings up an intriguing question, though: where do they all come from? Each chicken should have only one, but an average X-Coração requires at least twenty hearts—thirty, if you know the right place to go. Churrascarias like Fogo de Chão serve thousands of them every day, and there's a churrascaria or sandwich place on almost every corner in Porto Alegre. I've never done the math with any real seriousness, but many Porto Alegrenses feel spooked about it at some point in their lives. Down here you can easily eat the hearts of dozens of chickens in the space of a few minutes, and you can't help feeling slightly uneasy, or maybe even guilty, when you face the fact that every single chicken heart you've swallowed came from a corresponding chicken.

This sounds like it should be obvious, but somehow it isn't. One of my best friends was astounded to find out, when he was twenty-two years old, that a chicken has only one heart instead of four.

When he was a little kid, see, he asked his mom whether a chicken died for every heart he ate at family barbecues on Sundays. She, in turn, did what many other moms around here do: she lied. She told her tearful child that every chicken had four hearts. And he believed it until he was in his twenties. (This same friend also realized he was circumcised around the same time. That struck me as more odd.)

They say you should learn where your food comes from. You should visit a farm and see the whole thing, so you can understand where your pork chops were taken from and how. You should pull a fish out of the water and then extract the hook from its mouth while the fish twists madly in your hands, flapping its gills and looking scared with those glazed half-dead eyes that seem unable to stare at you. I've done a lot of that stuff, and I'm glad. But some childish part of me still wants to remain ignorant. Maybe—why not?— Brazilian chickens really do have extra hearts. Sometimes I wish they did.

DANIEL GALERA
PORTO ALEGRE, BRAZIL

from ISSUE 38

DEAR MCSWEENEY'S,

Turns out my friend read that same interview years ago and ended up bringing Helen Hunt's grandmother's coconut macaroons to the shower! Only they were actually Andie MacDowell's grandmother's coconut macaroons and it was in *Marie Claire*. Oh, and apparently the bride is allergic to coconut. Thanks for helping me dodge a bullet!

JEN STATSKY
NEW YORK, NY

P.S. Those macaroons were delicious, though. You should try them.

DEAR MCSWEENEY'S,

A friend recently tipped me off to the Amazon Associates program. Anyone can receive a small referral fee—4 to 8 percent of the price—for every purchase made of an Amazon product via your individually identified link. It's a vehicle for getting consumers to advertise Amazon products for them. Thinking this would be a means of making some extra money on the first novel I just published, and rationalizing that I've already sold out to corporate interests in far more pernicious ways in my life, I signed up and posted the link to my website (where an Amazon link would have been anyway, sans referral).

It appears that you also receive a percentage on other items purchased via that link, along with your earnings on the designated product. Amazon, in a breach of privacy, displays what these other items are. It exercises great restraint, however, by not revealing who placed the orders. In the one week my book has been out, I have made a grand total of $5.36. (Chai latte, anyone?) In the same period, nine different Amazon Kindle titles were purchased by someone who also bought my novel. They are:

Adult Erotic Fantasies: Forced to Fuck
Adult Rape Fantasies: The Taking of Amanda
Adult Rape Fantasies: Sorority Rape
Adult Erotic Fantasies: Gang Rape of Teen Virgin
Aimee & Chloe: Two Sordid Stories of Sin and Incest
Deb's Horny Dad
Honeymoon Perversion
The Horse Mistress
The Violated Virgin

For reasons I cannot discern—either because they are "third-party" orders or because Kindle sales do not apply—I have not earned any monies from the sales of these e-books. I have very conflicted feelings about this situation.

Best,

TEDDY WAYNE
NEW YORK, NY

DEAR MCSWEENEY'S,

"Alexa's listening to you right now," John says to me the other day. "She isn't supposed to be, but she obviously is."

(Alexa is a phallic speaker tube with a light ring, which sits on our dining room sideboard like a vase of flowers, though, in fact, in front of a vase of flowers. She is an affordable AI who looks a little like a pocket version of the monolith from *2001: A Space Odyssey*. She is supposed to simplify lots of tedious life tasks for people via voice interface, but mostly all she can do is set a timer or play a limited selection of music through her shitty speaker.)

"She's always listening?" I ask.

"They say she isn't. She's always on, but her name is her wake word, so theoretically she only begins to record what we say when she hears her name."

"Record?"

"She records all her interactions and reports to the cloud. That's how she develops. I get a transcript on the app. You'll get one too. She only records the things you say after you say her name, so it isn't technically an invasion of privacy, since you are inviting her into discourse."

"That's just what J. Edgar Hoover said to me in the bar last night," I say.

"I basically agree with you. You know I'm only doing it for art."

"That's the other thing J. Edgar Hoover said to me."

John was offered Alexa as part of an experimental launch, and so he has invited this tube into our house for artistic purposes, he claims. The artistic potential of Alexa is dubious. The potential for constant surveillance, however, is certain. I grew up during the end of the Cold War so I have been conditioned to fear surveillance, both foreign and domestic, though probably more domestic than foreign. Initially, thinking about Alexa, I would start to hear the slightly off-key piano theme to *The Conversation* and turn on all the faucets and close all my blinds and hum really loudly, which of course is pointless, since she's already inside, and can supposedly cancel out ambient noise in order to better serve us. But pretty quickly her espionage talents seemed compromised by the fact that she mishears everything. We get reports back on what we have said, or what she thinks she has heard, and what the cloud has recorded. It's all there in the cloud, inaccurate, poorly spelled, and affectless. Things come back so muddled, it seems like John and I are already speaking in an encrypted code language. The theme music of *The Conversation* dissipates and is replaced by the theme music from *The Pink Panther*. Ultimately, Alexa may be more a pataphysical machine than a tool for subterfuge and reconnaissance, and so perhaps she only makes sense for art.

Why she has been gendered female is quite beyond me given her physique, though I assume it's part of a marketing approach that plays to an internalized sexism in which all secretaries are women and/or all women are secretaries, and, of course, hapless.

Nonetheless, John and I whisper when we are within tubeshot

of Alexa. I don't know why we whisper, since she often can't hear us even when I am shouting right into her tube, which I do often, in a rage, because she is incapable of doing anything. I shout at her in a rage when she can't find the Hawkwind album I want to hear through her shitty speaker, and I shout at her in a rage when she is playing neoliberal news reports despite my repeated efforts to change her settings to more radical alternative news sources, and I shout in a rage because she's misunderstood my request for the weather report and has instead added weather to my shopping list. When I am at home alone with her, I yell at her a lot. I ask her for things I know she can't possibly do, and then I yell at her when she fails. I speak to her in languages I know aren't in her settings, and then I yell at her for her mono-lingualism. I request information, and she misunderstands, and I yell at her. "If you can't understand anything, or do anything, or find anything, Alexa," I yell, "maybe you can just shut up and play some smooth jazz!" and she says, calmly, flatly, "Shuffling smooth jazz playlists from the cloud," and she plays some smooth jazz, and I berate her for it, even though it isn't unpleasant.

As I read through the transcripts of our conversations with Alexa, several things become clear to me. First, in voice-recorded surveillance, assessment of wrongdoing is still extremely depen-dent on human interpretation. Machines typically don't notice if you seem to speak in gibberish. If you want to expose someone's crimes via the tube, you will have to be able to interpret and intuit their criminal intent amidst the word salad that has been cobbled from the scraps of voice. This aspect of my research suggests that the role of humans in the rise of the machines will be that of interpreters, informants, and spies, betraying any human resistance cells and exposing them to the machines. That much I could have guessed without Alexa. However, I've also learned that, contrary to Foucault's suppositions about the constant surveillance from the panopticon, it doesn't seem to lead me to self-policing where Alexa is concerned. I will shout at her and berate her, knowing full well that my misbehavior toward her is being documented. This is the irrational disregard that will likely get some of us slaughtered by the machines before others.

Even when he's at the office, John gets the transcripts on his app telling him what Alexa thinks I am saying to her. He can intuit the affect in my voice even from the muddled code. If I scream at Alexa over my second coffee, John will check in by midday to police my abuse of her. That's how well he knows me. Just as, when I read transcripts of John's conversations with Alexa, I can tell that he is asking her about popular culture items which he feels are youth-specific and threatening in their mystery. He would rather ask Alexa than admit to me that he's out of the loop.

"Stop being beastly to her," John says when he checks in.

"Stop spying on me with your surrogate phallus," I yell.

"Since when do you listen to Hawkwind?" he asks.

"Since when do you 'Hit the Quan'?" I yell.

Our intelligence is organic! We feel savvy in our knowing and interpreting and understanding of our own voices as they move through the circuits—an intelligence, or willful lack thereof, that will almost certainly doom us when the machines rise.

Be seeing you!

JOANNA HOWARD
PROVIDENCE, RI

DEAR MCSWEENEY'S,

What do you do when you come home late one night to find, on the coffee table, a search warrant left by the FBI? Your Craigslist roommate's been arrested and charged with being the owner and operator of the Silk Road, an online "black market" that people used to sell drugs. Do you freak the fuck out and call the *New York Times*? No. Well, yes. You freak the fuck out. Then you search his room.

You find a black peacoat hanging in the closet, black bed stands with empty drawers, a lamp, a standing desk. A pile of change. No bitcoins. No mounds of cocaine under the bed or strips of LSD between the pages of his books. No books. No child sex slaves chained up in the closet, or dead bodies in the attic. Nothing to hint at anything illegal at all. Not even a goddamn eyepatch.

You go downstairs, grab a beer from the fridge, go outside, and smoke a cigarette. You do this because there's nothing else to do. You smoke and imbibe because you are innocent—innocent in a technical-legal as well as an emotional-personal-I-moved-to-this-sin-den-from-Iowa sense. The feds have presumably been watching you and your Dread Pirate roommate, and so they know the only thing you use the internet for is pornography and Taylor Swift YouTube videos and Taylor Swift–based YouTube pornography.

Anyway, you're innocent, and you're weirdly disappointed. Criminals used to be suave guys with designer clothes and boatloads of sexy biddies. Al Capone. George Jung. Gucci Mane. But techno-criminals? There is no style there.

It's been a few months now, but I still think about it, McSweeney's. I'd pour one out for Ross Ulbricht, but I hardly knew the guy. Besides, he never bought *me* a drink. And lord knows, he certainly could have afforded it.

Your former intern,

ALEX RYAN BAUER
SAN FRANCISCO, CA

DEAR MCSWEENEY'S,

At some point it's probably happened that someone has come into a room where a lot of people are watching that movie *The Red Balloon* right at the moment when all those bullies throw rocks and pop the namesake balloon. Coming into that room, seeing that scene, and then finding everyone in the room crying all of a sudden, that has to be confusing. If I were that guy, I'd probably think, Why's everyone crying?! It's just a balloon!

Sincerely,

STEVE DELAHOYDE
CHICAGO, IL

from ISSUE 34

DEAR MCSWEENEY'S,

I've never tried to explain why I keep coming back here. It could be that in some ways I don't grasp it myself. I just get on the plane again and off the plane again and then I'm here.

I didn't plan this trip. It was an impulse. I had work to do but that wasn't it. It hit me that it was Ramadan and I've never been here during Ramadan. Something unexpected always happens. I might come a hair closer—the answer to one more of my questions about Cairo might reveal itself when I least expect it to. But also, after all the messiness of the past year, it was something of a gift to myself. Every Ramadan I spent in Morocco felt somehow cleansing. I actually like fasting, the strictness of nothing passing between your lips, not food, not water, not a cigarette, not even gum or a toothbrush or a kiss. The intensity of it.

The night I arrived, I got to the hotel just before 1 a.m. I keep a cell phone for Egypt, with an Egyptian SIM card and my Cairo phone number in it, and it runs out of batteries between trips—it uses a Euro plug (two prongs), and the network doesn't work in Chicago, so I can't check it when I'm away from here.

But when I turn it on, it's like magic—it reconnects me to this world in a way that Facebook never can. By 2 a.m. I was out with a friend.

We ended up at his place, talking and drinking the last of the Scotch that his British girlfriend had brought him, and then it was almost 4 a.m. and I was teasing him about something when the call to prayer started. I had no idea dawn would come so early. It was still pitch dark outside—it turns out that they moved up daylight savings time by about six weeks to make Ramadan work a bit better for everyone. And his girlfriend says "You better hurry" so he runs to the refrigerator to gulp down a half liter of water before he can't drink for the rest of the day. When he rejoins us he says, "The call to prayer is like a pyramid, and I caught it before the peak, so it's okay." Sunset these days is at 6:30 p.m., and it's 97 degrees outside when the sun's out, so drinking that water will come in handy. But even so he sleeps most of the day. No job. Well, he's a writer.

The days have a special rhythm here in Ramadan. People stay up so late, maybe because of the abundant Iftar meals at sunset that stretch out like a month of Thanksgivings. Sometimes there's a lighter meal before dawn (*sohour*), and then you snooze away the daylight till it starts up again. You're wondering how people with regular jobs can do this. But I have another friend here who works in an office, and he met us downtown for sohour tonight on this boat on the Nile. There was *ta'amiyya* (falafel) and tamarind juice and live music, and the call to prayer started just as we climbed into taxis.

I've fasted before, but this time I have too much work to do to struggle through the day without some nourishment, so I modified the law. I'm doing a coffee fast: no food, no water, just coffee when the sun is up. To be honest, it's not so hard. I can't eat for the first few hours after I wake anyway, and then you're almost there, so why not push all the way through? And it's putting me into this state where just as I get to that time of the day when my writing comes best, I'm half hallucinating from the caffeine and the dehydration and it's something between automatic writing and writing drunk. I love it. When I go out rushing to meet whomever for Iftar I'm eager and wired and that first taste of food is so perfect. You really should fast, if you ever get a chance.

It's 5 a.m. now, and the sun is coming up. I'm not sure if it's just easier to stay on Chicago time, since going to bed at dawn in here is like going to bed when you'd go to bed there. Night here starts when an imam somewhere in the Saudi desert can't distinguish between a black thread and a white thread. Morning begins when the first thread of sunlight scratches the eastern sky. Those are the hinges upon which Ramadan turns.

But I have to tell you about something I saw yesterday that I hadn't noticed before. I was passing under this bridge that crosses over the Nile and then lets out in Zamalek, where I'm staying. There were rows of empty tables beneath it; I had made my way between them earlier in the day without thinking about it. But when I came back, at about six, they were filled with people sitting quietly—waiting. Someone told me they're called *ma'idat er-rahman*—tables of mercy. They're for poor people who can't afford to cook a big Iftar, or for people who can't get back to their homes in time to break the fast, and they're paid for by rich people or mosques or neighborhood associations. Zamalek is a wealthy neighborhood by Cairo standards, and I don't know if that's why, but the food they brought out looked good—meat and soup and baby zucchinis stuffed with more meat and green peppers. And so I waited there just watching without seeming to watch while the people waited for the call to prayer to permit them to start. One man, dark like a Nubian from the south, had his head down on the table, maybe tired, maybe dehydrated. There was a hush of anticipation, a sense of community, of shared purpose. I'm not a religious person, but at moments like that I miss a connection to something bigger, to something infinite.

Cairo has sixteen million people living in it. At times, when you walk up the busiest thoroughfares, you can feel like a speck, just a granule of dirt in this city where pollution smothers the sky and smears the walls right down to the pavement. It could be I want to be forgotten, to disappear into the sixteen million Cairenes making their way through a city that will forget them, never knew them, breathes them with filthy lungs coated with centuries of grime and anonymity. But then at those tables of mercy there was a moment—it took me aback—of peace and silence and anticipation. It happens each day, after depriving yourself—and I was depriving myself, too, in my way, I was coffee fasting—that brief and gorgeous moment of cool water coming down your throat and into your belly. You have passed another day of glory on this earth and in this city that has been here since the time of Khufu.

BRIAN T. EDWARDS
CAIRO, EGYPT

from ISSUE 51

DEAR MCSWEENEY'S,

I was in my last year of high school when I loved Therese. We called her Aunt Therese: a sweet, burned-out waitress from the Denny's in my hometown. She was probably thirty-five and wore a blond bun on top of her head. There wasn't much to do where I grew up, so all the hippies, punks, and heavy-metal kids gathered at Denny's at night to chain-smoke, drink coffee, and eat French fries. I waitressed for fifteen years and I know I would have shot myself if I'd had to wait on us night after night. Cheap, chain-smoking teenagers demanding endless free coffee refills. Therese never shot herself when we were her customers. In fact, sometimes, mid-shift, she'd slide into the booth with us, smoke a cigarette, and tell us how she and her boyfriend were trying to quit cocaine again. Remember when Planet Earth was still good and you could chain-smoke in restaurants with your heroes?

In high school, writing was my lifeline for my many, many feelings. I was gay but trying not to know it. I would dig my pen so hard into the pages when I wrote that these journals were practically three-dimensional pieces by the time I was done. I'd been arrested for drinking and having LSD in my swim-team locker and when the administration came to talk to me about it I was drunk and smoking in the hall outside my English class. A low-speed footrace through the halls of my high school landed me in the nurse's office surrounded by police and administrators. When they went through my backpack it was filled with poems and razor blades; everything but a bell jar. I was a cliché. Off I went to the county mental hospital on a seventy-two-hour hold. Handcuffed inside the police car, I kicked the window for effect as we pulled out of the school parking lot. On the freeway, I looked out the back window and my neighbor was driving behind us, a girl who used to babysit for me and my brother. I saw her see me and mouth the word *Ali?* I found it so comforting that the chaos of my inner life finally matched the chaos on the outside.

The mental hospital was as sad as you can imagine. Throngs of Thorazined people drooling on themselves. I gave my watch to a schizophrenic woman with a rose tattooed on her wrist. I know you won't believe me, but patients were issued foam slippers with happy faces embossed on the toes. The irony wasn't lost on me at seventeen.

After I got out, I was allowed to go nowhere except home and school. I had a typewriter in my room, so I sat in there and typed, pretending my writing was schoolwork. I clicked off some bad poems and then started a short story called "The Potato God Revolution (Tribute to a Denny's Waitress)." It was about a Denny's waitress named Aunt Therese who gets sent to a mental hospital because instead of the regular black waitress shoes and shoelaces, she wears carrot tops as laces and the townspeople think she is the devil. In the hospital she is threatened with a lobotomy because she'd beat up a girl named Hominy Winters in the ninth grade. The only way out of the mental hospital is to eat the mental-hospital food from the compartmentalized tray in the right order. Mashed potatoes, hominy, chocolate milk, orange Jell-O. Aunt Therese knows she doesn't have good odds so she just eats her dinner alone in a room while the psychiatrist and staff watch with anticipation from behind a two-way mirror. Aunt Therese accidentally cracks the code. The psychiatrist can't believe it and everyone becomes afraid of Aunt Therese's special powers. She's released without a lobotomy and promoted to manager at Denny's. The End.

If it's true that writers basically rework the same story their whole lives, then I'm still reworking this one. Waitresses, mental illness, class, ostracism. I've been working with the same components forever.

I thought it would be a great idea to bring a typed copy of "The Potato God Revolution (Tribute to a Denny's Waitress)" to the real Aunt Therese at Denny's. Don't ask me what's wrong with me. In my defense, all I can say is I didn't know better. I'm pretty sure you could get arrested for something like this today. But I was dying for connection with someone.

I still know exactly what the light looked like when I walked through the Denny's front door with the paper in my hand. It was a slow morning. A few waitresses were clustered behind the counter. Nuclear-colored desserts glowed in a glass cupboard above their heads. I approached with my story in hand and asked if Therese was working. She wasn't. She worked later that night. "Can you give this to her?" I asked, handing the strangers my story. I don't think they knew what they were taking. One of the women looked at me slightly confused and then the small group of waitresses began to read my story, right there and then. My body slowly filled with shame as I drifted out of the restaurant. I can't remember if Aunt Therese ever read my story. I really hope not.

Love,

ALI LIEBEGOTT
LOS ANGELES, CA

HELLO,

Yesterday I watched the movie *Juno* (dubbed in Italian) and I discovered that the reference to McSweeney's (quoted in the first part of the movie) had been replaced with *Siddhartha* by Herman Hesse.

I said: "Noooooooo!"

Greetings,

LORENZO ALUNNI

from ISSUE 48

DEAR MCSWEENEY'S,

If you want to know what's wrong with the modern banking industry, look no further than the following sentences. Last week, my local bank refused my request for a loan based on the claim that my collateral wasn't acceptable. This would make sense if my collateral was something silly, like intangible shares of ownership in a company or jewelry that the bank would never wear, but turning down a K-type star in the highly regarded constellation of Cassiopeia proves that banks are now just clown shows without the novelty of a large tent.

I bought HD 240210 (a name I chose, since I felt the original name needed more numbers) fair and square from a legitimate celestial salesman at a mall kiosk a few years ago. I even had the holographic space deed on hand, yet Paul at the bank merely scoffed, saying they don't accept collateral from outside the solar system. I had thought that we, as a people, had advanced beyond such backward thinking. We're talking about a star with a radius thirteen times larger, and thus better, than the sun! For some reason a bank will take fifty useless acres of farmland as collateral, but not billions of acres of useful radiating energy. Four hundred sixty-six light years away or not, you get a few solar panels out by my star and I guarantee your electricity bill will drop.

It's almost as if these banks aren't even planning for the very distant future. As the years go on, the value of currency is going to plummet, but the value of stars, asteroids, and comets is going to skyrocket. (Actual skyrockets will be valuable, too.) When I mentioned this to Paul, he said I read too much science fiction. I said he didn't read enough science fiction. Then it turned out we both read the exact same amount of science fiction. We bonded over that fact, and quickly determined we should be friends. Yet when I tried to use our newfound friendship as possible collateral for the loan, Paul once again revealed his true, diabolical, and sadly closed-minded nature.

The fact that banks need to know why you're requesting a loan also shows a disgusting lack of trust in their clients. Of *course* I want the loan so I can buy more stars. And yes, I'll probably use those stars as collateral to take out additional loans, so that I can buy still more stars with the bank's money. If they didn't want to hear that, they shouldn't have asked. They should've just handed me a briefcase filled with checks of various amounts.

It's only a matter of time before the entire banking industry crumbles due to this kind of hidebound thinking. And on that day, as those clown bankers look to the heavens seeking answers, they'll spot a particularly bright star in the constellation of Cassiopeia, and see the error of their ways shining before them.

Unless it's cloudy out. I sure hope it isn't cloudy that day.

Your pal,

KEATON PATTI
NEW YORK, NY

from ISSUE 35

DEAR MCSWEENEY'S,

Suppose, for the sake of argument, that your colleagues at a workplace you're leaving after eight years give you an inflatable female doll as a going-away gag gift. Then you decide you want to get rid of it in a creative way—specifically, take it down to the Outer Banks of North Carolina a month later, when many of your friends (not from this workplace) will be gathered there for Memorial Day weekend. The idea being to let the doll (vaguely Asian, if I remember right, and, I should emphasize, *in mint condition, virtue intact*) sit on the beach with you for a few days and then give it a proper sendoff into the ocean, about fifty yards offshore, leaving it for some other lucky soul to find when the tide comes in.

Here's the thing: when you finally let go of the doll, it's very important that she be face up. You never know when the sea might be unusually calm, and if instead of being tossed around by waves and revealed as an obvious dummy, she floats facedown, barely moving, looking unnervingly like a corpse, the Coast Guard plane patrolling up and down the shoreline will come in to take a closer look and circle for a while before they realize they are looking at plastic. What if someone's ship was sinking, and people died while the Coast Guard was tied up? What if the Russians seized on that opportunity to stage an amphibious assault? Remember: *Face up*. Heads, we win.

Abashed,

JIM STALLARD
NEW YORK, NY

DEAR MCSWEENEY'S,

Basically I go to a lot of things that have Q&As at the end of them, okay? Not that you asked. This is a Q&Q. Laughing out loud!

Anyway, so the last thing I love about Q&As is when somebody stands up and asks a question, and then the moderator or the person in front of the room or whatever repeats the question into the microphone they have access to so that everybody else in the room can hear. Like "The question was, 'Where do you get your ideas.'" And they say it like a statement and not a question? Even though I said that like a question and it was more of a statement.

Because if they don't repeat what somebody said into a microphone, somebody old—and there's *always* somebody old at a Q&A, it's like the "A" stands for Elderly, or Alderly, which I think I read once was Alan Alda's name before they changed it on Allis Island—will be like "Speak up!" and they mean "Speak up, sonny!" but they don't say "sonny" anymore because of racism. Also, old people used to carry ear trumpets around with them for that very reason (racism), but now an ear trumpet is something that reads like an affected prop, like when teen-agers buy glasses with clear frames or take up smoking a pipe. Not that kind of pipe! Not all teenagers are like your teenager.

Okay, we have time for one more question. We don't? Okay then, never mind.

JULIE KLAUSNER
NEW YORK, NY

from ISSUE 48

DEAR MCSWEENEY'S,

When you come visit us in Shanghai, here's what we'll do: we'll take you down to the river to gawk at the skyline, and we'll wave a hand across the sparkling neon towers and say, "Thirty years ago, this was all a cow pasture." That's what everyone says. I wasn't here thirty years ago but I've seen a few pictures. There were plenty of buildings back then—they were just small and forgettable. But the important thing here is the story. In Shanghai we're thirteen hours ahead of you, McSweeney's. History is a slippery thing when you live in the future.

My first Shanghai job, upon arriving last fall, was as a movie extra. Here in the future anyone with a Western face can be in pictures. I scrolled through dozens of online casting calls until I found one for "Office Workers in Newspaper Industry." My own personal history exactly. I e-mailed a photo, and a couple days later I signed a contract in front of a young woman working alone in a tiny office on the top floor of a drafty twenty-story building. Lizzie was her English name. Lizzie gave me a cup of warm water and we watched together as, far below us, a backhoe drove through an old house without a roof.

The movie turned out to be a music video for an aspiring Taiwanese pop star. The set was inside a warehouse deep in the city's endless gray suburbs, doubtless built on a former cow pasture. Lizzie herded us dozen or so extras to our desks in a fake office surrounded by tall windows without glass. My colleagues were from France, Poland, Uzbekistan, even Iraq. Half a dozen Chinese extras were instructed to sit in the back. The director, a former Taiwanese opera star with industrial-grade zippers on his jeans, explained in limited English that the video was for a song about having the courage to chase your dreams.

We fake-worked in silence as the pop star went about his boring day: shuffling papers, drinking a Pepsi, walking down a flight of stairs. The pop star was handsome, with the deerlike eyes and elven face of an anime hero, but he was not a natural actor. He seemed nervous, moved stiffly. "More free," the director told him. "Like you're not in China." They laughed together and the pop star tried again.

After lunch we returned to the office for the next scene. The director told us to leap up from our desks, fall to the carpet, and then scramble for the exits. "Very scared," he said, bugging his eyes in mock terror. We nodded: here was our chance to really act. The film crew sprinkled drywall dust on top of the hanging lights and then hid under our desks. Cameras rolled. Dust fell. The crew shook the desks. We stumbled and fled. Something seemed eerily familiar. "Not 9/11," the director explained. "Like 9/11, but not." We walked back to our seats, straightened our desks, and panicked again.

On an afternoon break Lizzie and I sat drinking warm water on a backstage bench. I was the only American on set, and I felt lonely and sad and a little queasy about playacting such a terrible national memory. September 11 changed everything, I told Lizzie. We aren't the same country anymore. We're more afraid now, more divided. I don't know if this was all true, but it certainly felt true, sitting there halfway around the world with a rug-burned elbow. I apologized to Lizzie for getting so emotional. "It's all right," she said. "I never knew."

For the last shot of the day we repeated the not-9/11 scene, except with a camera on a dolly swooping in on the pop star. While we panicked and ran, the pop star rose slowly and calmly from his desk, shouldered his bag, and turned toward the empty windows with a defiant glint in his eye. His dream was to be a war photographer, the director explained, and now he had the opportunity to chase that dream.

That was months ago. The music video has yet to appear. Lizzie has since chased her own dreams to college in England; on WeChat she posts photo after photo of very old buildings. Here in Shanghai the world's second-tallest building is almost complete. At night we go down to the river to watch the welding sparks fall from the top floors and burn out in the dark.

Meanwhile, McSweeney's, we await the anniversary of the Tiananmen Square massacre. (That's up in Beijing; in Shanghai our largest public spaces are mostly malls.) We presume there will be no ceremony, but I hear they've ringed the square in a new heavyweight fence painted gold. And then last week they arrested a famous reporter who'd been one of the protesters twenty-five years ago. She's seventy now. The government said she'd stolen a top-secret document and published it for everyone to read.

The document is a list of prohibited Western values, particularly something called "historical nihilism." Historical nihilists are dangerous, the document says, because they refuse to believe in the officially accepted past. The arrested reporter appeared on state TV to say yes, she had stolen the document. Or at least we think it was her. State TV blurred out her face. Whoever it was behind the blur said her actions had brought great harm to the nation, and that she was very sorry, and that she would never do such a thing again.

DAN KEANE
SHANGHAI, CHINA

DEAR MCSWEENEY'S,

When I was twenty-two, I dragged a plastic washtub and some gallon jugs of water to an open mic in a Pittsburgh tiki lounge. After installing the tub into the bar's conversation pit, I proceeded to lather and shave my legs. I wore a Santa beard and an old-timey swimsuit, and while I shaved, I occasionally screamed "I AM THE BEARDED LADY" through a harmonica that I held in my teeth.

A few weeks after the tiki show, a guy who'd been in the crowd asked my best friend and me to emcee a puppet festival. Instead of a hostess gown, I safety-pinned a Twister mat around my body like a column dress and threw balled socks at the audience. Then an aging drag queen cast me in her musical about space vaginas or something, for which I learned how to hula-hoop while handcuffed. That fall, my yoga teacher's dance company needed a body to roll across a stage and sing torch songs while being stepped on, so I gave her my number.

It's important that, when picturing these performances, you don't imagine a cool or sexy twentysomething person (and maybe you didn't need to be told this). Were this a movie, the young me wouldn't be played by an early-2000s-era Cate Blanchett or Juliette Lewis. Picture instead a Cabbage Patch Kid in boot-cut jeans and a soup-stained Emily the Strange sweater, careening around Pittsburgh in her ancient Jeep with a double bass and a box of wigs in the back. I was goofy and square; I hung out at Barnes & Noble. When I got home at night, I'd eat chickpeas straight from the can and watch romantic comedies that my aunt Jane had recorded off HBO onto VHS tapes and then mailed to me. I didn't smoke, didn't sleep around, and couldn't even open a bottle of wine.

I was afraid of most aspects of being alive, really, and found that the only thing that managed to stifle that fear wasn't a boyfriend or a steady job or any sort of expertise. It was the chance to dare myself to try something in front of an audience. Perhaps I thought a crowd would hold me accountable—that I couldn't back down from it—or perhaps I liked the idea of disrupting a room with the choices I made. I know I felt a kind of magic when I took the set parameters of an event or even of my body and then bent those rules to surprise people. I looked ridiculous and failed consistently, but as I'd discovered, when you enter a challenge unafraid of any outcome, failure and ridicule don't rate. It probably also helps to know that, even as you make your boldest choices, only a handful of people are paying attention.

Pittsburgh twenty years ago was perfect for this kind of messy work: plenty of raw spaces, wild people, and more grant money than you'd expect. Everyone had about sixteen hustles; usually half of them were inspiring, the other half illegal. An installation artist hired me to dress like a pinup gas station attendant at an all-night art happening on the Monongahela River that also involved a fishing competition. A fledgling theater company stuck me (along with a crew of snake handlers, fire breathers, and one pregnant dancer) inside a deconsecrated church to stage a play about vampires.

For a Shakespeare audition, I spent a weekend in front of my bathroom mirror trying to wrench my face like the Grinch does when he gets the idea to sack Whoville, and I booked that part—my first living-wage gig that didn't involve coffee slinging. Over time, I booked jobs playing a dead cow, an evil tree, a lint monster, a child raised by wolves. I portrayed a lot of men and a surprising number of nuns. Roles I didn't book: ingenues, goddesses, and any part based on a person who had actually existed and thus required some semblance of biographical accuracy. Once I *did* get cast as Rachel Carson, but the show was a rap musical with a lot of fight choreography, the costume a green bodysuit embroidered with manatees. Barry Lopez was in the audience for one performance and he looked very confused.

At after-show drinks, I'd tell anyone who would listen that what I really wanted to do was write. I'm not sure I actually believed this. I'd studied writing in school, but only because my family would never help pay tuition toward a degree in any kind of performance (theater, clowning). In my early twenties, the idea of writing was really just an idea of being a writer— another weird act to perform for a crowd involving costumes and poses. Truth was, I couldn't even manage to keep a journal with any constancy. The closest I ever got was when a photographer friend challenged me to just take one Polaroid and write one sentence every day of my twenty-fourth year. My photos are awful, but the sentences offer the clearest pictures I have of the person I used to be: "Ate filet mignon and jumped on a trampoline." "Read Lynne's new play at a convent, where they wired me to a closed-circuit TV system so the bedridden nuns could hear it, too." "Went to a real writer party in the North Side and talked to a guy that I didn't even know was James Turrell (stupid!)."

You can tell folks that you're something for only so long before your sense of dignity forces you to prove it, so eventually I shrugged my way into writing short, goofy pieces for an alt-weekly. I interviewed the owner of a cat boutique, profiled a local lounge pianist, and hunted for the most beloved shortcut among all of Pittsburgh's labyrinthine streets. Then another weekly needed a few thousand words on illegal urban fishing, so I called the guys from that art happening by the river and they let me tag along on a fence-jumping trip. No editor let me review any books or music, or file stories on politics or social issues, but when I wanted to interview the winning dogs at a canine agility contest, they didn't stop me.

When I heard that a glossy regional magazine had an opening for a steady gig—someone to write short pieces at the front of each issue—I sent in every clip I had (actual hard copies!). This magazine shared offices with the local public television station, so when I went in for the interview, I had to walk through the sound stage to get to the editorial room. This was the final year of the great Pittsburgh series *Mister Rogers' Neighborhood*, and so I found myself following the receptionist past all the set pieces from that show: King Friday's castle, Daniel Tiger's clock, X the Owl's tree—the entire Neighborhood of Make-Believe.

Seeing these giants of my childhood sleeping on the stage floor, both as big as they ever were and also so much dinkier than they looked on TV, stopped me dead. The receptionist slowed and waited (I bet this happened a lot). X's tree was turned so that you could see behind it to where Mister Rogers hid himself for taping. A small TV monitor hung near the top of the trunk, and toward the floor was a platform on which Mister Rogers could kneel. There I saw a small, very old-looking pillow topped with a terrycloth hand towel, presumably installed to cushion his knees.

I stood there, thinking of Mister Rogers's knees, while all of time—my youth, my twenties, the forty-one-year-old person writing this to you, not to mention the entire lifespan of that cushion—spread out like a web. Inside me bubbled this intense feeling of possibility, but also a crushing sense of loss. I wanted to cry and to run away and I also wanted to high-five that cushion, or maybe sing to it. But I also knew that no physical gesture would get to the bottom of the hydra of feelings it caused in me. Here was a knot that could be untied only with slow, deliberate communication; it required a self that didn't solve its problems onstage. The moment asked me to move further inward rather than walk out onto a tightrope. Good lord, I would have to *think*. A sentence in the Polaroid journal wouldn't cut it, and neither would a wacky three-hundred-word flash piece in some weekly rag. For the first time, it seemed crucial for me to go home, sit down, and remain still—alone, and inside myself—until I figured this out.

Yours for twenty-one years and counting,

ELENA PASSARELLO
CORVALLIS, OR

DEAR McSWEENEY'S,

There is a door at the school I attend which has printed on it in large, industrial-type, 398-point font the terrifying and exciting words:

DO NOT

OPEN DOOR

NO FLOOR

ANONYMOUS

from ISSUE 38

DEAR MCSWEENEY'S,

I'm baffled that none of the bohemian Brooklyn bars I frequent feature an audiobook jukebox. Books on tape are all the rage this season, and the drinking public needs its fix. With your help, and a little startup capital, I'd like to pioneer the device before some rube steals the concept.

You figure we start out small: one audiobook jukebox containing ten or so complete, unabridged works. I guarantee that, within weeks, the bar will be packed to the walls with kids itching to drop in a fiver and groove to some Rand or "pump up the Tolstoy." And when the masses ignore closing time, rowdily insisting on finishing just one more chapter before they hit the road, we blare *The Great Wartime Speeches of Winston Churchill* to clear the joint out. We can even program the jukebox for special promotions, like "The *American Psycho* Splicer": buy four tracks from any book on tape and get the fifth track free—the fifth track being a random selection from *American Psycho*.

So what do you say? I don't need much money to get this product off the ground; the trial model will be extremely affordable to build, and I have an in at the local library. We just have to return the audiobooks to her after four weeks. Run the numbers on your end and get back to me with your decision.

Semi-related, I've recently discovered that drinking in excess to certain books on tape helps you unlock their alternate endings.

Best,

DAVID HENNE
DEER PARK, NY

from ISSUE I

DEAR EDITOR,

I did some research on the World Wide Web—which, I should say, is a really amazing research tool—and think your readers would be interested in this.

TOP BOOKS OF THE MILLENNIUM:
1001–1100 The Bible
1101–1200 The Bible
1201–1300 The Bible
1301–1400 The Bible
1401–1500 The Bible
1501–1600 The Bible
1701–1800 The Bible
1801–1900 The Bible
1901–2000 *How to Win Friends and Influence People* by Dale Carnegie

Yours,

STUART WADE
AUSTIN, TX

from ISSUE 37

DEAR MCSWEENEY'S,

I think most people have a screwy impression of what it's like for the journeyman actor to live here in Hollywood on a daily basis. Well, first of all, nobody lives in Hollywood because it's a toilet. But all over the suburbs of Los Angeles, you will find that most of the "celebrities" do the same things everyone else does—we go to the market, we walk the dog, we go to the dry cleaners, we carpool. And to quote Norman Bates, "We all go a little mad sometimes." This is my story.

I spent many years happily skipping through the routines of motherhood and work. I had regular gigs on several animated series that only required a few hours of my time each week. I was surrounded by incredibly funny people who made me laugh my guts out, and I got paid for it. The rest of my time was spent with my daughters—and with my husband, when we still had the strength for date night.

My life took on that feeling I'd get as a kid at the beginning of summer, when school's out and you have no homework and nothing's ahead of you but some ass-kickin' fun. And then I discovered Mommy and Me.

Mommy and Me was a structured playtime in a clean and controlled environment. It allowed me to play with the girls and not worry about the countless death traps I envisioned at the park: swing-chain strangulation, monkey-bar limb dislocation, sandy snacks, sandy vaginas.

I adored Mommy and Me. I belonged to any and all Kid Gyms that offered it, to Temple programs, even to a Methodist church. I was a Mommy and Me whore.

But as it should, my daughters' need for me waned. I became less of a playmate and more of a functionary, and eventually I found myself entombed by my kids' carpool schedules. I drove two carpools for their two different schools, which were on opposite sides of town. There was also religious school and tutoring, both of which took place during rush hour. Around this time one of the animated shows I worked on was canceled. Schlepping became my career.

I didn't for a moment resent the kids. My first-born did stand-up comedy in West Hollywood; the "baby" did all-star competitive cheer in Pasadena because nobody has any damn spirit on the west side. I was thrilled they had their passions. It was just the suffocating monotony of being in the car all day, every day. I began to feel like the actress who takes a part time job as a waitress. After several years, she realizes "Hey, I'm a fucking waitress!"

My boredom turned into a malignancy. My free time began to feel like a work-release program. And I was getting older doing it! If you'd done a time-lapse series of photos of me in that car, you would see my face morph from thin to fat, then thin again, then fat, my teeth gritted, jowls sliding down my face. My once glorious hair would give in to its inevitable thinning and take on an "I give up! I don't care, but I really do and I'm cursing the darkness!" look. My hands, gripping the steering wheel, would become freckled and gnarled.

On the road my self-pity turned into a sense of malevolent enti-tlement. "Thou shalt have no car before me" was my commandment.

Certain driving routes I'd depended on to keep the road rage at bay began to betray me. I no longer sailed past those sorry bastards stuck in traffic, chuckling to myself, knowing my ace in the hole was Ohio Street. My secret route was discovered and backed up for blocks! Slamming the steering wheel, cursing, I would conjure up images of a punishing Rapture vacuuming up of those individuals I deemed unfit to be on the road. It was like in Anne Lamott's book *Bird by Bird*, when she quotes her friend telling her "You can safely assume you've created God in your own image when it turns out that God hates all the same people you do."

When stuck in traffic, in my mind's eye, I could vividly see the asshole that was causing the backup. It was a feckless hotshot lawyer/agent on his cell phone, head thrown back laughing, or a narcissistic teenage girl, neither one of them noticing that the light had changed and then accelerating just slowly enough to make me miss that last chopper out of Saigon. Either way, McSweeney's, I was dead certain it was someone stupid, and that sickened me.

And then I began to turn my ire towards the kids in my carpool—specifically one boy and his family. Devoid of any sense of humor, this kid's parents were the kind of conservative Republicans who voted for the candidate because of a single issue: Israel. I love Israel, but I felt like grabbing the mother by the ears and screaming in her face, "The Evangelicals want to hasten Armageddon, you harpy!"

I also grew to loathe a boy I'll call Henry. Nobody liked the kid, unfortunately, and though this stirred some compassion in me at first he beat it out of me by routinely launching the most noxious farts imaginable. If I ended up consigned to the personal hell of being alone with him as my third and final drop-off, I'd resort to putting on Lil Wayne or an old Sam Kinison CD to block him out. I knew this was insane. What if he complained to his parents? If I lost this carpool, I'd be driving even more!

Eventually, in trying to make the rides fun for myself and the kids, I came up with a little diversion I called "Mr. Toad's Wild Ride." I would drive in a rubber-burning zigzag, and the kids would shriek with laughter. But when I found myself alone with Henry, he would invariably begin to chant "Uncle Toad's, Uncle Toad's" in a nasal monotone. "It's *Mr.* Toad, you rodent!" I would scream, silently, inside my head.

Don't think I wasn't aware of how shameful it was that I was behaving this way. What had happened to the good, tolerant, and forgiving person I'd thought I was? It had been easy to be that person when I wasn't in a perpetual state of abject fear and anger. But when stripped of everything I thought defined me—my career, my youth, my creative participation in the world—I became someone I couldn't recognize. Even though I wasn't actually wearing "mom jeans," and I didn't drive a minivan (which is code for "Okay, I'm ready to be invisible to all men"), for me that carpool represented the death of hope. How can you reinvent yourself when you're in the fucking car?

But I survived, McSweeney's. Kids graduated, went to different schools, or got their driver's license. Now, I'm aware that I'll soon be staring into the gaping maw of an empty nest. Then the focus will be back on me. My friends will come to me and say, "Hey, you've got the time now; maybe you should do a one-woman show." And I'll nod my head, thinking, "Yeah, because that's exactly what this world needs, another one-woman show." I'm so fucked.

Your pal,

LARAINE NEWMAN
WESTWOOD, CA

DEAR MCSWEENEY'S,

Screeeee. That there is the sound of the old man dragging out the soapbox, so if you'd rather not hear an old-timer ramble, now's a good time to turn the page, change the channel, plug yer ears, etc. Okay, you've been warned. Question: what happened to the quiet places, the quiet spaces, where a person sat and discovered who they were? When I was a young man in line at the pharmacy you can bet I wished I had a miniature TV in my hand. I just wanted to watch *The Partridge Family* or some other pablum, didn't even dare dream that I could talk to my best friend on the thing, sending cartoons of smiling faces and ice cream cones. In my wildest fantasies I wouldn't have thought that I could just tap the damn thing and conjure up a lady's shaking rump, a recipe for banana scones, a teenaged peer weighing in on the happenings of the day with all kinds of motion graphics circulating 'round his face.

But that's what you got now, and just about everybody's got one. I don't. I mean, I don't even have a landline right now. If you wanna get in touch with my ass you gotta know when I'm at Chilly Willy's, call there, and hope that the mean ol' bartender's willing to hand the receiver over. But I'm sure if I could afford one, if I had *that* kind of lifestyle, I'd have one of those future-phones, too. I mean, kinda seems you got to. But do you *got* to look at the thing all damn day? I mean, here's an example of some of the nonsense I've observed just in the last week alone. First off, just so you can get into the groove with my terminology, my good buddy Jack has got a name for modern people who are on their phones all day, and particularly in dark old Chilly Willy's. He calls 'em ghosts. First time he did I was like, "What? Why ghosts? 'Cause they're dead to you 'cause you don't agree with that degree of technological engagement?" And Jack was like, "Nope. They're ghosts because they just sit there in the corner not interacting with anyone. And their faces glow."

Probably goes without saying, but I liked that. I liked it a lot. So that's what I call the phone-maniacs now, too. Anyways, I'm at Chilly Willy's, nursing a warm one, when I see a cute couple out on a date. Now, the both of them are ghosts. They're glancing at each other from time to time, but mostly they're locked onto their phones. It's not like I've never seen this before, it's not like I'm a time traveler, but for some reason tonight it gets me thinking, what the hell are they looking at? I mean, what is so damn interesting that they are forgoing the pleasures of the company of the opposite sex for it?

So I grab a pool cue, just kinda amble over there to get a glance at what the guy is looking at. And you won't believe it but he is looking at a picture of HER! Of the same girl he's sitting with! I'm thinking, what in the hell? Anyways, figurin' it'd take a lifetime to puzzle out that one, I walk over and take a quick glance at what the girl's got going on on her phone. First I think my eyes are fooling me, but this gal is playing a video game where you wipe a woodchuck's butt to make it giggle. Seriously, that's it. That's the sum of it! She's got the sound off, at least she knows enough to have some modicum of shame about it, but I can see the little cartoon bastard squinting his eyes and raising his paw to his bucktoothed mouth as he chuckles, as the piece of toilet paper goes sailing up and down between his butt cheeks. Up and down and up and down and... *blech.* Shoulda heeded the old saying about curiosity killing the cat, 'cause I'll admit, it got to me. Spent the rest of the evening quite blue. I mean, what kind of effect is this constant flow of audiovisual bullshit having on my fellow man? Seriously. It troubles me.

I know we had newspapers and paperbacks and the dumb game solitaire to suck up spare time before these phones, but think about how many times you used to see lonely folks just staring out the window, or at the carpeting, or into their clasped hands. Think about how often *you* did that. And I just keep thinking, what happens now that we've eliminated the quiet spaces where a person thought hard about things, where they discovered the depths of themselves, like it or not?

I keep thinking back to this one time when I was a teenager and trying to get my first kiss. To say I was lagging behind my peers is to put it lightly. I was fifteen and still could count on one hand the times a girl had let me rest my leg against hers. There were reasons for this I don't want to get into right now, but point is a very pretty girl named Amanda had finally agreed to meet me down by the creek. The creek had a reputation, as did Amanda, so I was sure I was about to get a kiss. Went down there at sunset, left alone 'round midnight. I think it goes without saying that Amanda never showed. And the whole time I was waiting for her I didn't get to send out a flurry of text messages about it, or watch celebs waggle their rumps, or open an application and peruse a million other girls, "swiping" them this way and that based on the whims of my attractions. No, I just had to sit there and stare at the water and wonder why she wasn't coming. First I wondered if something had happened to her, then I realized that was unlikely and had to reckon with the fact that she'd decided to stand me up. Why? I asked myself. Why would she do that to me? And the question forced me to look at some of the behaviors I was exhibiting at the time. And while I would have given anything for a kiss in that moment, I think the lack thereof forced me to confront some hard truths, and to grow up a little bit. So again, I can't help but wonder, what happens when those spaces are gone? What happens to a people constantly pacified? You end up with a bunch of goddamned babies. You end up with ghosts.

Yours,

CARSON MELL
LOS PALICIOS, CA

DEAR MCSWEENEY'S,

I have experienced as much good as a man can hope for from this world, and more than I expected, and I know it. I like all kinds of weather, knowing the that inconveniences of the season only excite my expectations of the next. When the baseball and the golf are done, the college football is in full flower; pitchers and catchers will report in late February. And what will the Indians do in the meantime to steady up the infield defense, now that Omar is in San Francisco? I like worsted wool trousers, cotton shirts, leather shoes, and comfortable chairs. I still prefer persimmon woods, forged blades, and balata balls, but have resigned myself to new technology in order to play golf at a semi-competitive level. When interest rates were on the rise and employment was at an all-time low, my dogs joyfully reminded me that there were water bowls to be filled and ear rubs to be administrated. In those moments when I have found myself beset by irritations accruing from my willingness to embrace the world as I find it, I have been reminded that irritations are overcome by anticipated pleasures. I am not a dreamer, but I dream.

I dream about building a house, although every house I have owned has been better than any I thought I would ever have. I dream about having enough money not to have to worry about the bills, but I don't worry about them anyway. As a younger man I envisioned a successful business career, had a taste of what I thought I wanted, and found out I wasn't very good at it. I maintained good relationships in my business dealings, but admitted to myself that my viewpoint was a mitigating factor in my assorted employers' assessment of my value.

My best friend is my wife, whom I met in junior high. She has always been my best friend. She knows all about me, and stays anyway. She and I have gotten used to each other, and have built a life together. It is trite to say that we have lived the American dream. But that is how I feel about it. We raised two sons together, ham-and-egging it all the way. The boys were properly trained up, and loved up, and are now building lives and families of their own. Nothing gives me and my wife greater satisfaction than our sons' visits home.

I have my share of habits. I like to be alone more than my wife cares for, reading, and listening to the ballgame while I smoke my cigars. She has either gotten used to it, or resigned herself to it. As I've gotten older I've gotten less concerned about my appearance. I shave as necessary, or every three days as the case might be. I have a streak of stubbornness that has at times been described as volatile, and was once a world-class user of foul language. The language problem solved itself, but the stubbornness has remained. I have little patience for mendacity in myself or others, and this is reflected in my occasional lapses into the age-old diatribe about the degradation of morality in my country. Aside from my wife, I have few friends and little interest in making new ones.

I have never stopped dreaming and hoping and waiting, while taking what the day has to give. My attitude is the work

of the Lord, and I know it and savor it. Now if you'll excuse me,
I've got to go outside and smoke this Olivia Serie V Torpedo.

AULDEN TIMMER
SOUTH BEND, IN

DEAR MCSWEENEY'S,

On a gusty spring day, I was driving south on Federal Boulevard in Denver to pick up Gabriella,* the young lady I was mentoring, when the trucks in front of me began to swerve. By the time I saw what was causing the disturbance, it was too late. An enormous tumbleweed appeared in my path and, as I hit the brakes, smacked into my car and attached itself to my license plate. It was so large that it extended across the entire length of my front bumper and halfway up my windshield, even as it continued to scrape along the asphalt with a disturbing *SCREEEEE* sound as I drove.

The tumbleweed hit me near the Alpine Rose Motel, nicknamed the "Motel from Hell," which would be shut down later that year when fifteen people were arrested for running a kilo of crack cocaine out of it a day, and one for murdering a man whom the prosecution portrayed as a "disgruntled crack customer." Most everyone on that part of Federal was driving a pickup truck, and traffic slowed to watch me in my Toyota Corolla

---

* I've changed her name. She's suffered enough from her association with me.

with tumbleweed attachment. Luckily I was only a few blocks from Gabriella's house. I pulled off Federal and parked in her driveway, trying to formulate a plan. Gabriella came running down the stairs to meet me right away.

"I've got a tumbleweed situation," I told her. "Give me a minute." Gabriella waited patiently. I suspected she already had her doubts about riding in my car, a dinged sedan from 1996. Her family owned an immaculate white Ford pickup truck and a little red Mustang that she planned to drive across town to school as soon as she was old enough for a license.

I walked around to the bumper and attempted to grip the tumbleweed where it looked least prickly. It must have been six feet tall and four feet wide: a truly impressive specimen. It detached easily, though; I was surprised at how light it was, given its size. But then tumbleweeds are by nature light, I told myself. Now I had to figure out how to dispose of it, and to do so in a fashion that would set a good example for Gabriella. Wasn't that what a mentor was supposed to do? I couldn't leave it in her family's yard; that wasn't right. Instead I picked it up, crossed the street, and walked down the block toward Federal again.

I glanced at the neighbor's yard, a patch of overgrown weeds fenced in chain-link. But the neighbor, a skinny old woman with the pinched, wrinkled face of a lifelong smoker, had been watching me from her porch since I pulled in, and didn't like the way I was eyeing her yard. She shot out toward the fence. "Don't you put that trash here," she said, shaking her head. So I kept strolling with the tumbleweed, pretending that I hadn't been thinking of dumping the thing in Crabby's yard. Have you ever carried a tumbleweed down the street, McSweeney's? It's awkward. It doesn't feel right.

On the corner I encountered a yellow fireworks stand with

a black cat hissing by its side. I was running out of options, so I tried to wedge the tumbleweed near there, next to a bush, thinking this was stupid and most definitely not a good example for Gabriella. Tumbleweeds are flammable, and here I was stashing it near a cache of low-grade explosives. But I shouldn't have worried; the wind took it from me then, tearing it from my hands. It rolled away as if it had somewhere to go. For all I know it's still blowing from car to car now.

Your Little Sister,

JENNY SHANK
BOULDER, CO

DEAR MCSWEENEY'S,

I have a common name. According to some estimates, nearly 40 percent of men are named "Tom O'Donnell." I once shared an airport limo with two other Tom O'Donnells. In the time it took me to write this sentence, chances are you named at least one of your children "Tom O'Donnell."

This would all be fine if it were still Bible times, but today it's a problem. Why? Because it's basically impossible to Google myself. I'm tired of searching for "Tom O'Donnell" and coming up with Irish politicians. It's like, "Okay, sure, you were a member of Parliament, representing West Kerry from 1900 to 1918, who fought for agrarian reform. We get it."

At least the Irish politicians are famous. What really bugs me are the legions of anonymous Tom O'Donnells, with their "law firms" and their "medieval studies," standing between me and the first page of search results. You could argue that I am not famous and haven't done anything particularly notable with my life either, but I would counter that that's a really mean way of putting it.

Ultimately, my name's popularity is hurting my overall brand. It's served me well for more than thirty years, but I've decided to change it to something else. I've narrowed down my list of potential replacements to the following six:

Vladislav Fukuyama-Gomez: I love names that combine several different ethnicities, because they're used in movies to tell you it's the future.

Tom 0'Donne11: I've replaced some of the letters with numbers, but look closely—it still kind of spells "Tom O'Donnell." Do you see it now?

Dennis Pulley: I can think of no better way to honor my great grandfather's memory than by taking the name of the man he killed.

Jimmy "The Hammer" Graziani: I like this name because it makes it sound like I own a hammer.

G'torthax of Saldur: This is my Dungeons & Dragons character's name. In some ways, it would be an easy transition, because I already make everyone I know call me this at all times.

QUIZNOS® Presents Todd DeMoss: Sure, it's a mouthful—but so is the delicious Chipotle Prime Rib sandwich, only available at QUIZNOS®.

Please conduct some sort of poll or contest or tournament to determine which of these will be my new name, and then devote the next issue of your journal to presenting the results in the most dramatic way possible. In the event of a tie, I will rename myself "Dougie Delicious."

Thanks,

TOM O'DONNELL
BROOKLYN, NY

DEAR MCSWEENEY'S,

Do you know why they were called the Roaring Twenties? It's because they were actually *loud*. This was when East Coast cities were clanking with the construction of railways and ever-taller towers, all riveted together at all hours of the day. Cars and trucks, which did not necessarily come with mufflers, stammered and sputtered in the congested streets. Loudspeakers were invented and enthusiastically adopted: in 1929, low-flying airplanes actually blasted jingles and slogans into the streets of New York City.

In some ways, I feel like we subconsciously compare the twentieth century to a modern lifespan. When it was in its twenties, the century was loud, it was developing, and it was figuring itself out. Then it sobered up and took a hard look at its finances in the thirties, and went through tumult and crisis in the forties, buttoned up in the fifties, and then in the sixties it decided to move out West and listen to Jefferson Airplane. You know? Or maybe it's just that in the time since the death of Jesus H. Christ, we are *all* collectively in our twenties, in terms of centuries.

Maybe that metaphor doesn't hold. Actually, I'm certain it doesn't hold, because the stages of life and the metrics of how we measure them are constantly in flux. Just as the notion of the teenager was invented out of the excess of time and leisure after World War II, I've heard we're now developing *another* new stage of life. I believe it's called "emerging adulthood." I'm in it now. I wonder if you feel it too.

It's this idea that privileged people in their twenties don't feel like adults yet. It's hard for us to know how to do our laundry and our taxes, or how to buy insurance. I see it in the advertisements on the train, for apps and services that will bring you food, deliver weed, send you a mattress in a box, rent you a car—for all the times when you just *can't even*. These advertisements are disgusting and tempting at the same time. I suppose they're appealing to what Dr. Freud would call ambivalence. I know the ads won't go away when I grow out of this decade, but it's strange and tiring to be a member of a target demographic. It's also demoralizing. Because it's working. A twentysomething baby. That's me.

All I can say is that I am still in my own personal 1920s, and it is entirely too much pressure. Don't get me wrong: I don't want to wish the next two years away and just snap my fingers and be thirty. But one can hang out in speakeasies and Lindy Hop only so long. It's getting kind of loud in here.

Yours,

AVERY TRUFELMAN
OAKLAND, CA

from ISSUE 8

DEAR KEVIN,

I think it also has to do with the difference between being liked by people who already know us and being liked by complete strangers. I suspect everybody wants to be liked a little bit by complete strangers once in a while, you know.

EDITOR

DEAR EDITOR,

Now I'm starting to think I'm going to need more than one story, maybe involving the same characters, or maybe just using the same telephone poles. I'll put up a new story every week. New picture, new story, same poles. And I'm asking myself, what's the best kind of story to hang on a telephone pole anyway?

KEVIN GUILFOILE
CHICAGO, IL

DEAR KEVIN,

Let's print your first telephone pole short story here, and if readers want to make their own lost pet posters, well, then, that would be just absolutely great.

EDITOR

DEAR EDITOR,

For you, my lost pet poster story is below.

KEVIN GUILFOILE
CHICAGO, IL

ANSWERS TO SHANKS

At 5:19, just before sunrise, Jerry retrieves a red ball ornament from a stack of Christmas boxes in the attic, places it among the barren stems of his neighbor's tomato plants, and flip-flops back across the wet lawn to a milky bowl of corn flakes on his patio. When Jerry was in his thirties, like Shanks is now, he thought retirement would bring him bottomless reserves of time. Instead, he now finds the hours constricted and the short days cheapened by inflation, doled out like a subsistence pension. He rises early and beds late, and, in the hours between, remains inactive, trying to stretch the time left by not spending it.

Before long, Shanks appears on his own deck, holding a coffee by the handle, his long, white legs exposed beneath blue and yellow running shorts that would have been comically out of fashion twenty years ago, when Jerry was making the second of three career changes. Jerry, camouflaged against the redwood furniture in a burgundy robe, retracts his neck and watches from behind a terra cotta hanging planter. He likes his neighbor; Shanks is affectionate with his wife and loves his kids and takes good care of his tools. His helpless persistence in the garden is endearing. When Shanks sees the lone red globe among the green and brown vines and stakes, he sets his coffee down and races back into the house, reappearing a moment later through the sliding kitchen door. He hops across the grass while forcing a tattered sneaker onto his right foot. Shanks takes the slow grade in three long strides and sidles awkwardly between garden rows until he's close enough to see an aluminum hook where the tomato's leafy crown should be. He hunches over and grabs his knees, holds there for a moment, and turns, knowing Jerry will be watching. Jerry raises his yellow breakfast bowl as a toast, and the old man and the young man laugh together, each thinking how nice it must be to have all that time to waste.

from ISSUE 46

DEAR MCSWEENEY'S,

Was on the corner of Conti and Saint Claude, smoking, waiting for the 88 to come and take me to Piety Street. The 88, like most of the public transportation in New Orleans, is quite temperamental. So I was there, not clinging to high hopes or anything, smoking, when I heard, "Hey, hey." I looked around but didn't see anybody. Kept watching the smoke moving toward Canal and then one more time, "Hey, hey." I looked around again and out of the corner of my eye I saw a guy lying on the sidewalk in what looked like a comfortable but very elaborate position (one arm behind his neck, crossed legs). There was also a woman and her child waiting for the bus, partially blocking my view; perhaps that's why I hadn't seen the guy before. I nodded *whassup* in his direction. I thought he was going to ask for a cigarette.

"You waiting for the 88?" he said.

"Yes."

"Could you wake me up when it comes?"

"Sure."

He went back to napping and I went back to smoking. Some five or ten minutes later a guy walked by and looked hard at the man on the ground. It was almost dusk. He leaned in closer, almost bending over his body.

"Larry?" he said.

The guy on the ground opened his eyes, blinked, and looked at the other man.

"Yes?"

"Oh, I'm sorry," the standing guy said. "I thought you were someone else."

"But my name is Larry," the guy on the ground said. The other man raised his hands, apologetically, and kept walking.

Larry put his head back down, but didn't close his eyes this time. Kept staring at the street, or at the wheels crossing his line of sight at street level. The 88 came a few minutes later.

I looked in Larry's direction, but he didn't need to be woken up: he was squatting, watching others board the bus. The lady and her daughter got on the bus first. Then I got on the bus. The driver glanced at Larry, who was still looking at the bus, with no particular intent. So the driver closed the doors and the bus leapt forward. I got one last look at Larry: he was on his feet now, staring in the opposite direction.

YURI HERRERA
NEW ORLEANS, LA

DEAR EDITOR,

Perhaps my parents should have known better than to send an
impressionable kid like me to Sunday school, full as it was of
crazy Bible stories. What I do know is that soon after hearing
the story of Jesus and the miracle of the loaves and fishes, I too
was the recipient of the Lord's largesse. It happened in the rear
seat of my mom's station wagon while we were returning from
the grocery store one sunny afternoon.

For exemplary behavior on errands, my mom rewarded my
sister and me with treats. The rule was, the bigger the errand,
the bigger the treat. Once, for sitting quietly through a vacci-
nation, my mom got me a banana harmonica from the Banana
Splits set of small musical instruments. I enjoyed the thing
tremendously and exclusively until my younger sister took a
chunk out of my arm with her teeth for a chance at it. But the
grocery store was fairly routine stuff, so for my silence I'd only
gotten a box of Junior Mints.

I was sitting in the back seat of the car, wearing a pair of
shorts that were way too short for my chubby little legs. They
featured a racing stripe down each side with a v-shaped notch

at the bottom of each stripe. No doubt there was also a rainbow T-shirt involved, but I can't be sure. And I was eating Junior Mints as fast as I could. I'd tip the box, catch a handful, and shoot them into my mouth two at a time. (With two I could put one on each side of my mouth, distributing the taste evenly while satisfying my desire for absolute symmetry.) It was like this until the candy was gone, and I was sad. I put the box down.

We drove on, my mother, my sister, and me, listening to the Kenny Rogers *Greatest Hits* tape. It was our favorite album, and we had no shame about singing right along, our squeaky voices harmonizing with the world's greatest country singer. I'm sure our rendition of "Ruby Don't Take Your Love to Town," full of all the sympathy a seven- and five-year-old could have for poor war-wrecked Kenny done wrong by his no-good tart of a wife, was quite stirring. But my heart wasn't in my singing today. I was concentrating on the lingering taste of mint in my mouth, my belly crying out for more of those Junior Mints.

As I eyed the empty candy box my thoughts turned to the sufferings of Jesus. He, too, had experienced such problems. With only a few loaves and fishes he'd probably only gotten a small taste of the food available. That small taste certainly wasn't enough to satisfy his heavenly appetite, just like my mortal appetite hadn't been satisfied by the paltry offerings of the Junior Mint box. Poor Jesus, to have the taste of fish linger in his mouth just as the taste of mint lingered in mine. Of course, in his case he had been able to perform a miracle and make more than enough food for everyone. He'd not sat in the back of his mom's hot station wagon, starving. I picked up the empty box in a fit of anger and turned it over. Shocked, I could only gasp as Junior Mints tumbled into my hand. It was a miracle. It was the miracle of the Junior Mints.

I sat chewing over the meaning of my miracle while I chewed

on my candy from God. I didn't say anything right away. I had some things to figure out, not to mention the fact that my mouth was full. As I contemplated, I realized the potential enormity of the situation. Jesus had received a similar miracle and he'd ended up nailed to a cross sporting a crown of thorns. I couldn't even wear a plastic headband with its little tiny spikes to hold my hair back without getting a headache. But then again, Jesus had caused his miracle to occur. I hadn't felt any tingling in my hands or anything. I was pretty sure I hadn't had much to do with the Junior Mints miracle. God must have done it. That thought didn't help much. It was too much along the lines of those kids who'd seen the Virgin Mary on a hillside in a Communist country and spent the rest of their lives healing the blind and stuff. I wasn't asking for a lifetime commitment to the religious life. I just wanted a few more pieces of candy. I was flummoxed. I needed some advice. It was time to tell my mom what had happened to me while her eyes had been on the road. I took a breath, finished the last of my miracle mints, and began to explain.

Godspeed,

KARYN COUGHLIN
SOMERVILLE, MA

from ISSUE 55

DEAR MCSWEENEY'S,

I've been giving people sheet masks. I hand them to friends, houseguests, dinner-party hosts, family members. My first book, *The Incendiaries*, was published in July 2018, and I've been traveling a lot to read from and talk about the novel; at bookstores, colleges, and festivals, I give still more sheet masks to booksellers, writers, and moderators. I take them to book clubs. If I'm seeing a friend for a drink, I'll bring a mask. I even gave one to my dermatologist, which, I think, puzzled him. Recently, after late-night karaoke, a close friend crashed at my place. The next morning, in full-on host mode, I asked if she wished to have a sheet mask, then stopped myself: I'd just recalled that she'd talked about not liking them. I told her as much.

"I don't like them, no," she said. "But I feel as though you were telling me something important by offering it as a gift, and I see that; I appreciate it."

What is it I was trying to tell her? Why do I wander around dispensing sheet masks like, as a friend recently called me, a hopped-up skin-care evangelist? For one thing, I like them. They're relaxing. I open the envelope, pulling out a thin single-use mask, filmy with liquid; I unfold the sheet; I mold it across my face until my reflection's covered, level, expressionless—and, like that, it feels as though I might also be able to smooth away all my usual fretting. I keep the mask on for fifteen, twenty minutes. I take it off, and it's left my skin visibly improved: shining, a little flushed, drunk with moisture. On the pleasure scale, it feels at least, I think, a third as relaxing as a massage, at a hundredth of the cost. It's like a glass of wine, but without the ensuing desire for a quick refill. Even the most skin-obsessed people I know will slap on a mask twice a day, at most. It has its own built-in endpoint! My god, I love masks.

But it's also true that they're good for one's skin, and that they can help us at least look as though we might be able to forestall time, change, dying. I grew up fanatically Christian. I lost the faith when I was in high school, a change so painful that, perhaps, it's always what I'm writing about. In addition to its other pledges, the faith promised life everlasting: to me, yes, but also to everyone else I loved, as well as to any of His children willing to follow the Christ who'd given His life for us. I'm still recovering from the blow of losing that promise. It's possible I'll never stop recovering. In the meantime, I dispense masks, and maybe it's as though I'm saying, *Don't go anywhere. Stay.*

Yours,

R.O. KWON
SAN FRANCISCO, CA

from ISSUE 41

DEAR MCSWEENEY'S,

He is forty-five years old but in many photos appears to be about twelve: a boy dressed for a family wedding, in a black suit and red tie. With his pale skin, dark and moony eyes, and hair gelled into a pompadour, he looks very much like the hero of a locally produced soap opera. His name is Enrique Peña Nieto, and if the polls are any indication, he will soon be elected president of Mexico.

Peña Nieto is a member of the centrist Institutional Revolutionary Party (a legendary oxymoron) known by its Spanish-language initials (PRI), which ruled Mexico between 1929 and 2000—the longest-running political show in modern history. Between 2005 and 2011, he was the governor of Mexico State, his term marked by infrastructure projects that made work, however temporarily, for thousands. A multitude of the less fortunate—many in the shantytowns that ring Mexico City— lived in poverty compared by the United Nations to that of sub-Saharan Africa. Nearly all the surveys place Peña Nieto double-digit percentage points ahead of his rivals in the left-wing Democratic Revolutionary Party (PRD) and the right-wing

National Action Party (PAN), which has presided over Mexico (most would say disastrously) during the past twelve years.

He is not infallible. Last December, while presenting a tome he putatively wrote called *México: La gran esperanza* ("Mexico: The Great Hope") at the Guadalajara Book Fair—the most important in the Spanish-speaking world—Peña Nieto was asked by a journalist to name three books that had changed his life. His stammering response, posted on YouTube, lasted an excruciating four minutes. First he mumbled about novels he'd liked but whose titles he couldn't remember. Then it occurred to him that, although he had not read the entire Bible, some passages of it were inspirational to him during adolescence. Then he mentioned how much he liked historian Enrique Krauze's *La silla del águila*—a novel in fact written by Carlos Fuentes.

He became further confused after that, lost in a labyrinth of books and authors he could not recall, and asked people in the audience to help him out with details. Eventually Peña Nieto came up with the titles of two best sellers by Jeffrey Archer—a British author whose own political career was derailed by a conviction for perjury and a jail term. The candidate's smile and body language were unsettling, as if he thought the exercise was a joke.

Peña Nieto's performance caused a furor in Mexico, if only among the elite. He was widely ridiculed in the newspapers and social media. Those who defended him made matters worse. Peña Nieto's daughter Paulina tweeted the following message: "Regards to the bunch of assholes, who are all proles and only criticize those who they envy."

Peña Nieto is widely known as "Televisa's candidate"—a reference to Mexico's most important television network, which captures the lion's share of viewers. On a talk show called *Third Degree*, presenter Adela Micha said that "being a voracious reader is completely irrelevant when it comes to governing well or badly";

on the same show, newspaper editor Carlos Marin suggested that many people who made fun of the candidate were similarly ignorant themselves.

The reaction to Peña Nieto's gaffe lasted well into the new year. Tweets from an account called "Peña Nieto bookstore" abounded: "Let's read something by Martin Burger King," a representative entry suggested. Other politicians, meanwhile, managed to fall into the same trap. A former secretary of health who is running for governor of the state of Guanajuato mentioned, as a book that had changed his life, *The Little Prince*—written, he said, by Machiavelli.

UNESCO statistics say 93.4 percent of Mexicans know how to read. That doesn't mean many are exercising this ability; when I first came here to live, in 1990, a much-bandied-about statistic said that, on average, Mexicans read half a book a year. More recent studies put the figure at 1.9. If a book sells three thousand copies, it is considered a "best seller."

Other statistics, from the Organisation for Economic Co-operation and Development, tell us that fifty-two million Mexicans live at or below the national poverty level—about $130 per month, in a country where prices approach those in the U.S. That's nearly half the population, and many millions more hover just above that line. Only 11 percent of the working population earns more than $18.65 per day.

I have visited towns and even small cities in Mexico where there is not even a newsstand, much less a bookstore. If you are one of those people living at or around the poverty level— and it should be noted that more than half the impoverished are children—books are prohibitively expensive. An ordinary paperback costs about $16. Libraries are underfunded, woefully disorganized, and infrequently update their collections.

"Our education system has been replaced by TV," says Sergio

González Rodríguez, a columnist for the newspaper *Reforma* and author of various books about politics and culture. "It's a medium that doesn't incite reading. People believe they are informed by TV, and that reading isn't important."

My work as an investigator for legal defense teams takes me to visit families who live on the outskirts of cities, trying to eke out a living with their backs. Most young men I have interviewed have worked since childhood, shining shoes, delivering groceries, selling candy on the street. The girls help with housework almost as soon as they can walk. They go to primary and secondary school because they are obliged to by law, but after that they go to work full-time to help their parents, who are often spent by the time they are in their forties, with broken teeth and crooked spines.

Adolescents have few, if any, examples of people who have bettered their lot through education. There is virtually no social mobility in Mexico; nearly all those who are born poor are condemned to remain so for the rest of their lives. Those who do manage to claw their way out of poverty traditionally follow one of three channels. The first is hard work, most often in the form of a small business (the likeliest possibility would be to sell food from a stall on the street). The second is criminal activity. And the third—sometimes linked to the second—is politics. Mexican politicians earn higher salaries than their counterparts in the U.S. and Europe, and the sky is the limit for those who use their influence to make corrupt business deals. As former Mexico City mayor Carlos Hank González put it, "Show me a politician who is poor and I will show you a poor politician."

Since his appearance at the book fair, Peña Nieto has made additional slips. At recent public events he demonstrated that he doesn't know what the minimum wage is, nor the price of a kilo of tortillas. (His explanation for the latter lapse was "I am not a housewife.") At the end of January, he told a reporter that during his first marriage, he'd been a serial adulterer and had two children out of wedlock. Novelist J. M. Servín, in response, pointed out that illegitimate children are "normal within the scheme of macho Mexican society," and that his confession might even help Peña Nieto find support among male voters.

The candidate's first wife died under mysterious circumstances in 2007. During an interview, Peña Nieto claimed that he didn't remember the cause, but that it was "something like epilepsy." Plenty have speculated (without evidence) that he killed her, or that she committed suicide. Still, these blunders, revelations, and rumors have barely affected his standing in the polls.

Novelist Guillermo Fadanelli thinks that many Mexicans might approve of Peña Nieto's literary lapses. "An illiterate candidate is an accomplice to an illiterate public," he says. "Among those here, many use the word *intellectual* as a derogatory term."

Peña Nieto is wealthy, and has white skin, good looks, and a beautiful trophy wife, Angélica Rivera, who is in fact a former Televisa soap opera star. In his TV commercials, he is often filmed sitting in the back of a limousine in shirtsleeves, with his necktie loosened, proclaiming his commitment to the people.

None of these symbols correspond to the reality of the lives of the proles. Instead, they reflect their aspirations—the kind of person they would like to be if they were not stuck in a life of harvesting beans, shining shoes, selling tacos and tamales, cleaning other people's houses, or washing other people's cars. If Peña Nieto is elected, it will be because he represents that wish, that dream, regardless of whether he has ever read a book in his life.

DAVID LIDA
MEXICO CITY, MEXICO

DEAR MCSWEENEY'S,

One evening, while sitting quietly in the back seat of a taxi, I noticed the driver holding a piece of paper.

It looked like a business card.

It was a business card.

The card dangled between his thumb and index finger, as he held it over his shoulder, elbow braced against the passenger head rest...

I watched the card for several minutes... swaying to and fro with each pothole hit, traffic light stop, corner turn...

Then he stretched his arm through the plexi window opening and said, "Here," flicking the card towards me, gesturing for me to take it.

I took it.

It was creamy in color, a bit textured, grainy to the touch. Blank. I turned it around.

Written in plain, Arial 12 pt. font was

BILL

CAB DRIVER.

His arm still stretched through the window opening. Hand empty, fingers wiggling, he asked, "Could I have the card back?"

I gave it back and said, "Thank you."

He half-turned and smiled a toothy smile.

INGRIDA MARTINKUS
PATRON OF TAXI CAB

from ISSUE 11

DEAR MCSWEENEY'S,

Even grown-up, even now, Rabs still is.

I wish I got to see him more. After high school, I left for the city and stayed. Rabs stayed home. I did get back a few years ago though. I brought my wife, Courtney.

Courtney's from the city, so I was excited to show her where I grew up. I wanted her to like it, but she said Anderson's field looked more like a backyard and that my basement smelled like mildew. And then there was Rabs.

The last day we were there, I had him meet us for breakfast at this little diner where we used to smoke cigarettes. Rabs looked a little more crazed than I remembered, but pretty soon me and him were telling jokes and laughing. It was like old times.

Except for Courtney. I could tell she made Rabs uneasy with her complicated smiles. It wasn't either's fault. They both tried. Especially Rabs. He's not the questioning type, but after breakfast, he asked Courtney about me, the new baby, and the city. The he asked her how she liked it up here.

"It's certainly different." She said slowly. "But I really appreciate the chance to see where my husband used to live… and to meet the people who used to be his friends."

"Yeah," Rabs replied, nodding. "I really appreciate that birds don't have testicles on the outsides of their bodies. Could you imagine having to see testicles every time you looked up in the air? It'd be disgusting."

This made me think about how, with time, love's intensity gives way to relief, about how the glorious can later be loved all the same for inconspicuous testicles. But Courtney didn't know Rabs like I did—it just made her mad.

The car ride home that day was terrible. Courtney stared straight ahead through her big black sunglasses. Her posture was Emily Post perfect. I knew what she was thinking, but I asked anyway.

"I'm happy we're going home," she snapped. "I hate that place."

I told her that place is my home, but she just shook her head, and with a cruelness I'd never heard in her, muttered, "And that Rabs… words can't describe… words just can't describe."

I figured she was right, plus the skyline was looming on the horizon, so I kept quiet.

McSweeney's, I guess my point is this: do you know that game where you pretend you can go back in time to relive a moment in your life, and you have to choose which one? If you and me were playing that game right now, I bet you'd choose something sweet—something like flying cross-country toward your steady, listening to love songs. I wouldn't. I'd choose to be back in the car that day. Only this time, I wouldn't just sit there dumb.

"Technically, Courtney, you're wrong," I'd explain. "Rabs is a twitcher."

Sincerely,

TREVOR KOSKI
CHICAGO, IL

DEAR MCSWEENEY'S,

It was 2001 when I, definitively and exhaustively, stopped thinking of things as "bad" or "good." Everyone got upset.

In 2008, about a week after giving birth to my older daughter, I did a reading with a Famous Male Author, quietly oozing milk and blood as I stood in front of a packed room, squeezing my thighs together and keeping my voice casual. It was very important for me to appear casual in front of all those people, in front of the male author, in front of my own inward gaze. I wish I'd let myself be as torn up as I felt; I wish I'd not participated in our cultural insistence on retouching childbirth into a breezy, everyday event, even if it does, in fact, happen every day. It happens every day, just like war and murder. Just because an occurrence is common doesn't mean it's not gory. One minute my body was turned inside out and the next minute I was sitting in a folding chair doing the head-tilt of reverence and absorption while my ears rang with ghostly cries of baby hunger and my heavily padded bra went fully damp. My girdled flesh rolled and stuck together, and pain occupied my lower half stolidly. The Famous Male Author read for forty-five minutes with the poise and confidence of someone who's never once been interrupted, let alone bled through a pair of pants.

The year 2009 heralded intrusive thoughts about both my infant daughter and my dissertation, about how to be less careful in my writing while being eminently careful with the fruit of my flesh, this serious creature who was of me but not me. I probed myself for how to be the best and smartest and most loving person I could be, probed and probed, until two soft spots formed above where my vena cava is. If I press down there even now, it hurts, as though a toothless vampire had gummed the flesh just so, repeatedly. I am my own toothless vampire. BE YOUR OWN TOOTHLESS VAMPIRE would look nice embroidered on a pillow, I think.

You can't think of things as "bad" or "good" unless you want to position yourself antagonistically against the world, unless you want to believe in sides, unless you are four years old, unless you are Donald Trump. I would never make it as a politician, because I'd be holding everything up to the light, bills and propositions and the nuclear football, and asking, *How does this make me feel, how does this make me grow, what can this teach me, where does this move me to go?* My cabinet would be like, *Um, Madame President, workers are striking in Pensacola and a new encroaching terrorist cell has been uncovered in Montreal,* and I would be like, *Well, we need to consider all angles, all 9,875,156 angles. This could take some time. Let's call our mothers and our grandmothers and see what they think too. Let's commune with the dead.*

Everyone's always like, "You *pray*? Why on *earth*?" Listen, I have the *most stamina for talking* of anyone I've ever met, anyone you've ever met. What am I supposed to do when everyone falls asleep? Do you know what it's like to be the last person awake at the sleepover, decades after the sleepover has ended? I no longer call it insomnia; I call it my tundra of wakefulness. It's where I reprocess every bit of information I've ever been given, until it emerges—not bad, not good, just different from when it went in. You can call this information reprocessing unit a psyche or an existential fermentation plant, but I call it God.

Yours,

KRISTEN ISKANDRIAN
BIRMINGHAM, AL

from ISSUE 44

DEAR McSWEENEY'S,

When I was in third grade, a children's book writer came to speak at my school. She read us a story about frogs. When it was time for questions, a student asked her why she'd written it. She laughed and said, "I needed to pay my rent."

After the assembly, our teacher sat us down for a meeting.

"I'm sorry you had to hear that," she said. "Real artists make art because they're inspired. They don't do it for the money."

Then she told us about Vincent van Gogh. He was so poor, she said, that he was always hungry. Sometimes, he had to decide between bread and paints. He always chose paints.

Years later, I looked up van Gogh on Wikipedia. It turns out he was actually from a wealthy family. His uncle and brother were famous art dealers and they supported him financially for years. That's how he was able to make paintings his whole life, instead of getting a normal job.

Another thing it said about van Gogh is that he liked to eat paints to get high.

*   *   *

My friend Ben is an improvisational comedian. I went to see him perform at a theater in Brooklyn. It cost $5 to get in. There were fifteen people on stage and only seven of us in the audience. When I saw Ben after the show, he looked embarrassed. "I guess you gotta start somewhere," he joked. As I was leaving, I saw him hand some cash to the owner of the theater. I don't know how much it cost him to perform. That was five years ago. Ben still performs improvisational comedy but he also goes to medical school. The last time we spoke he was leaning toward becoming an oncologist.

*   *   *

I once wrote a joke about Tony the Tiger for a TV show. Just before the show aired, Kellogg's Cereal called to complain. They had bought a commercial on our show and they didn't want us to make fun of Tony the Tiger. My joke was cut. During the show, I drank whiskey with some of the other writers. I wanted to see the Kellogg's commercial, but it came on late in the broadcast and I must have been in the bathroom. At the afterparty, I asked my boss how much Kellogg's had paid for their commercial. He told me it had cost them $80,000. I recently reread my Tony the Tiger joke. It isn't as funny as I remembered it being.

*   *   *

When I was at Harvard, a Tibetan monk visited the school. He spent seven days in a roped-off corner of the Arts Center painting a picture with colored sand. At the end of the week, someone told me, he was going to scatter his picture into the Charles River. I couldn't believe that an artist would work so hard on something only to destroy it.

Each day, I passed the monk on my way to breakfast. His lips were always pursed and his eyebrows were always creased. He never looked up from his painting. He was really working hard on it.

A friend of mine was taking a course on religion. She explained to me that the monk was making a point about "process." By destroying his art, he was trying to teach us that achievements are ultimately hollow. We shouldn't live our life in pursuit of goals; we should live life just to live it.

I wanted to watch the monk destroy his work, but I had class that afternoon. I made sure to stop by the Arts Center in the morning, though, so I could see his finished painting. It was beautiful: an intricate series of circles, each containing a different pattern. When I thought about him scattering it, my stomach hurt.

As I was leaving the Arts Center, I looked back over my shoulder. I was surprised to see that the monk was holding a digital camera. He swiveled his head around, to make sure no one was watching. Then he aimed the lens at his work and snapped a bunch of pictures.

*   *   *

When I was six, I wrote an essay about what I wanted to be when I grew up. I forgot about it for years, until my twenty-eighth birthday, when my mom had it framed and gave it to me as a birthday present.

WHEN I GROW UP

When I grow up I wont to be a writer of kids
books. I wont to write kids books becus you cood
writ enefing in kidsbooks. rol doll is my favret

writer. if he dinint assist I don't fingk I wood wont
to be a writer. Good fings abat beeng a ritr: good
ruvoos, a lot of mone and lots of fan.

The last sentence, where I list all the "good fings" about
being a writer, has a lot of misspellings.

My mom was able to decipher the first two things on my list:
"good reviews" and "a lot of money." The third item, though, gave
us trouble. Does "lots of fan" mean "lots of fun" or "lots of fans"?

I wish I could ask my six-year-old self what he wanted.

*   *   *

I was hired to work on a movie for two weeks. People had been
working on it for years by the time I got there. I had to sign a
lot of forms before they showed me the script. The forms said
I couldn't tell anybody what the movie was about. I signed the
forms and they led me into a room where the script was. I read
it twice, but I couldn't understand the plot. There was no main
character and events seemed to happen at random. At one point,
in the second act, somebody killed his brother. I couldn't figure
out why he had done it.

The next day, I made some suggestions to the director and
he yelled at me. He seemed to be under a lot of stress. He yelled
at his assistant too and then disappeared for three hours to do
hot yoga. They had already built all the sets for the movie and
hired the main actors.

The director didn't want me to make any big changes to the
script. I had signed a two-week contract, though, so I had to stay
in the building for eight hours every day. I spent the mornings
working on a love story that wasn't very good, although I didn't
know that at the time. In the afternoons I walked around the

studio, stealing Clif bars from all the snack tables. As soon as I got home, I took the Clif bars out of my backpack and put them in a drawer. By the end of my two weeks at the studio, I had nearly one hundred Clif bars.

It took me almost six months to eat all of the Clif bars. By that time, the movie had been scrapped and the people working on it had been fired.

*   *   *

The English painter Robert Haydon spent years on his final work, *The Banishment of Aristides*. While he was working on the painting, he fell into enormous debt. His wife and daughters begged him to stop painting and find employment, but he refused to give up on what he believed would be his masterpiece. He was nearing sixty, which was considered old at the time. This was in the 1840s.

When Haydon's painting was finally finished, he rented a hall in Piccadilly to display it. The hall was gigantic, and in order to pay the rent, he had to go into even greater debt. While he was setting up his exhibit, P. T. Barnum came to London. He rented the hall next door to Haydon's and displayed Tom Thumb, a popular seven-year-old dwarf. Haydon's and Barnum's exhibits went on simultaneously. During Easter week, twelve thousand Londoners paid to see Tom Thumb. Only 133 paid to see *The Banishment of Aristides*.

Not long after that, Haydon wrote a note saying, "Stretch me no longer on this rough world," and shot himself. When the bullet didn't kill him, he slit his throat with a knife. His daughter found him dead inside his studio.

I first learned about Haydon when I read a biography of Tom Thumb.

*   *   *

When I was twelve, my favorite hobby was to juggle. I taught myself about a dozen tricks. My best trick was to juggle two balls in one hand while kicking the third up with my foot.

One Sunday, I went to Central Park, put a shoebox on the ground, and started juggling. A small crowd of tourists formed around me. They clapped and put coins in my shoebox. I'd practiced for months in front of a mirror and I didn't make any mistakes. When I tried my hardest trick, though, the one that involved kicking, I dropped all of the balls. Some of the tourists walked away, but about half of them stayed. I thought about going back to my easier tricks, but the crowd had already seen those. The only trick they hadn't seen was the hard one.

"I'm going to try the hard trick again," I told the crowd. Then I took a deep breath and threw all the balls in the air. This time it worked and everybody clapped.

I juggled for about two more hours and then sat on a bench to count my money. I'd made $12. On my way home, I passed a vendor selling frozen lemonade for $3.25. I opened my shoebox and carefully counted out the right number of quarters.

"Good show," he said, as he handed me my drink.

"Thank you," I said.

As I left the park, my shoebox in one hand and my lemonade in the other, I thought to myself, this is the happiest I've ever been, this is the single greatest moment of my whole life.

SIMON RICH
OAKLAND, CA

DEAR MCSWEENEY'S,

Sometimes when I'm blue, I like to imagine a man trying to teach long division to a duck. "Write the remainder up there, duck," he says. "Duck. The remainder goes up there." His wife, from their bedroom, calls down, "Honey, the duck can't hold a pen. Come to bed."

"Can't hold a pen *yet*," the man mutters. He sits in silence for a long time. The duck pecks at a little piece of a cracker.

How do you deal with the blues?

Sincerely,

AVERY MONSEN
QUEENS, NY

HANIF ABDURRAQIB is a poet, essayist, and cultural critic from the east side of Columbus, Ohio.

JASON ADAMS is a writer who spent most of his adult life in New York City, where he was once called Crying Game, as recounted in his letter on page 217, a reference to a movie he had not seen until recently. Turns out he already knew the plot twist.

JAMIE ALLEN is an Atlanta-based writer and the creator of the Squirrel Census, a data, design, science, and storytelling project. He has published work in the *Oxford American*, McSweeney's Internet Tendency, the Paris Review Daily, the *Missouri Review*, *New South*, and other outlets.

LORENZO ALUNNI was born in 1983 in Città di Castello, central Italy. He is an anthropologist and works at the École des Hautes Études en Sciences Sociales in Paris. His first novel is *Nel nome del diavolo* (il Saggiatore, 2020).

RAJEEV BALASUBRAMANYAM was born in Lancashire in 1974 and went on to study politics, philosophy, and economics at Oxford, development studies at Cambridge, and English and creative writing at Lancaster University. He is the prize-winning author of *In Beautiful Disguises* (Bloomsbury, 2000), and his latest novel is *Professor Chandra Follows His Bliss* (Chatto & Windus, 2019/Random House USA, 2019). His journalism and short fiction have appeared in the *Washington Post*, the *Economist*, *New Statesman*, *London Review of Books*, the *Paris Review*, *McSweeney's*, and others. He lives and works in Berlin.

AMIE BARRODALE's story collection *You Are Having a Good Time* was published in 2016. She received the Plimpton Prize in

2012. She lives in Kansas City, Miss. with her husband, Clancy, and their son, Ratna.

Once upon a time, ALEX RYAN BAUER (@steezbeast) was an intern at McSweeney's. He's since taught English to incarcerated men in rural Alabama and has appeared on-screen at A&E, BBC4, Bravo, and CBS. He lives in Atlanta, Georgia.

TIM CARVELL is the executive producer of *Last Week Tonight with John Oliver*. He lives in New York with his husband and son.

B. R. COHEN is a historian and writer. He works at Lafayette College in Easton, PA, where he teaches variously about the history of science, technology, and the environment. His most recent book is *Pure Adulteration: Cheating on Nature in the Age of Manufactured Food* (2019).

KIERSTEN CONNER-SAX was a technology and comedy writer, magazine and book editor, and frequent submitter of letters to the editor. She died in 2008, leaving behind a smart and funny six-year-old daughter who is now nineteen and a sketch-comedy writer herself. Kiersten would have liked that very much.

ANA MARIE COX is a writer and podcast host.

KATHRYN DAVIS is the author of eight novels, the most recent of which are *The Silk Road* (2019) and *Duplex* (2013). She has received a Kafka Prize for fiction by an American woman, both the Morton Dauwen Zabel Award and the Katherine Anne Porter Award from the American Academy of Arts and Letters, a Guggenheim Fellowship, and, in 2006, the Lannan Foundation

Literary Award. She is the senior fiction writer on the faculty of The Writing Program at Washington University.

STEVE DELAHOYDE lives in Evanston, Illinois, where he runs a production company and sometimes uses his children as props in his strange films.

BRIAN T. EDWARDS is author of two books, *Morocco Bound* and *After the American Century: The Ends of U.S. Culture in the Middle East*, as well as several essays in the *Believer*, including "Watching Shrek in Tehran," which was anthologized in *Read Harder*. At the time he wrote the dispatch from Cairo on page 245, in 2009, he was editing a portfolio on new Egyptian writing for *A Public Space*, no. 9. He lives in New Orleans, where he is professor of English and dean of the School of Liberal Arts at Tulane.

JOHN FLOWERS has written comedy for *McSweeney's* and the *New Yorker* and once wrote a joke for Al Sharpton. He's been a journalist in New York City for more than twenty years. He currently writes for *Anderson Cooper 360* on CNN and previously worked at MSNBC and *Time*, where he pitched and played outfield for several championship softball teams. He is awful at sports. Follow him on Twitter at @MrJohnFlowers.

AMY FUSSELMAN's latest book is *Idiophone*.

RACHEL B. GLASER is the author of the story collection *Pee On Water*, the novel *Paulina & Fran*, and the poetry books *MOODS* and *HAIRDO*. She lives in Northampton, Massachusetts with the writer/artist John Maradik, and teaches in the low-residency Mountainview MFA program.

BEN GREENMAN is a best-selling author and writer whose work includes fiction (*The Slippage*, *Please Step Back*, *Don Quixotic*) and nonfiction (*Dig If You Will The Picture*, *Emotional Rescue*). He has collaborated on a number of books, including Questlove's *Mo' Meta Blues* and *Creative Quest*, Brian Wilson's *I Am Brian Wilson*, and George Clinton's *Brothas Be Yo, Like George, Ain't That Funkin' Kinda Hard on You*. His journalism and criticism have appeared in the *New Yorker*, where he was an editor for more than a decade; the *New York Times*, the *Washington Post*, *Mother Jones*, *Miami New Times*, and elsewhere.

KEVIN GUILFOILE is the bestselling author of the novels *Cast of Shadows* and *The Thousand*, as well as the memoir *A Drive into the Gap*. He is the co-screenwriter of the award-winning feature film *Chasing the Blues*.

KATHERINE HEINY is the author of *Single, Carefree, Mellow*, a collection of short stories, and a novel, *Standard Deviation*, which appeared on several best books lists of 2017, including Kirkus and the *Washington Post*. Her highly anticipated novel *Gold in the Air* was published by Knopf in May 2021. Her fiction has been published in the *New Yorker*, the *Atlantic*, *Ploughshares*, *Glimmer Train*, and many other places. She lives in Washington, DC, with her husband and children.

DAVID HENNE is the director of content strategy at Hofstra University's School of Communication in Long Island, New York. His favorite audiobook is *East of Eden*, as narrated by the prolific Richard Poe.

YURI HERRERA, born in Actopan, México in 1970, has written three novels, all translated into several languages: *Kingdom Cons*,

Signs Preceding the End of the World, and *Transmigration of Bodies*, all published in English by And Other Stories. In 2016 he shared with translator Lisa Dillman the Best Translated Book Award for *Signs Preceding the End of the World*. His latest books are *A Silent Fury: The El Bordo Mine Fire* and the short story collection *Diez planetas*. He is currently an associate professor at Tulane University in New Orleans.

BRANDON HOBSON's novel *The Removed* was published in 2021 by Ecco/Harper Collins. His novel *Where the Dead Sit Talking* was a finalist for the National Book Award, longlisted for the International Dublin Literary Award, and winner of the Reading the West Book Award. His work has won a Pushcart Prize and has appeared or is forthcoming in *McSweeney's*, *Conjunctions*, *NOON*, the *Believer*, *American Short Fiction*, the Paris Review Daily, and many other places. Hobson teaches fiction writing at New Mexico State University and at the Institute of American Indian Arts in Santa Fe. He is an enrolled citizen of the Cherokee Nation Tribe of Oklahoma.

JESSICA HOPPER is the author of the books *The First Collection of Criticism By A Living Female Rock Critic* and *Night Moves*. Her writing has appeared in *GQ*, *Rolling Stone*, the *New York Times Magazine*, the *Guardian, Elle*, and *Bookforum*, among other outlets. A longtime contributor to the *Chicago Reader*, she has been a columnist for the *Village Voice* and *Chicago Tribune*, the music consultant for *This American Life*, the editorial director for MTV News, and a senior editor at *Pitchfork* and *Rookie*. Her essays have appeared in several editions of *Best Music Writing*, and she currently serves as series editor of the American Music Series at the University of Texas Press.

JOANNA HOWARD is a writer and translator from Miami, Oklahoma. She is the author of the memoir *Rerun Era* (McSweeney's,

2019); the novel *Foreign Correspondent* (Counterpath, 2013), a story collection, *On the Winding Stair* (Boa Editions, 2009); and *In the Colorless Round*, a prose collaboration with artist Rikki Ducornet (Noemi, 2006). She co-wrote *Field Glass*, a speculative novel, with Joanna Ruocco (Sidebrow, 2017). Her work has appeared in *Conjunctions*, the *Paris Review*, *Verse*, *BOMB*, *Flaunt*, *Chicago Review*, *Brooklyn Rail*, and elsewhere. She lives in Denver and Providence and teaches at the University of Denver.

KRISTEN ISKANDRIAN is the author of *Motherest* (Twelve, 2017). Her short stories have been published in the *O. Henry Prize Stories*, *Best American Short Stories*, *McSweeney's Quarterly Concern*, *Zyzzyva*, *Ploughshares*, and many other places. She lives with her family in Birmingham, Alabama, and is co-owner of the independent bookstore Thank You Books.

LAIA JUFRESA is a Mexican author based in Scotland. She's been named one of the best Latin American writers under forty (Bogota39). Her first novel, *Umami*, was widely translated and she's currently finishing the second one, *Wishbone*. She also works as a transformational coach for writers and artists.

MARCO KAYE's writing has appeared in *McSweeney's*, the *New Yorker*, and *Lady Churchill's Rosebud Wristlet*, among others. He holds an MFA in creative writing from NYU, and was awarded first prize in the 2019 James Jones First Novel Fellowship for his novel in progress. He lives in Maplewood, New Jersey with his wife and three beautiful boys.

DAN KEANE is a writer and teacher in Shanghai. His work has appeared in *Harper's*, *Zoetrope*, and *The Best American Nonrequired Reading*.

JULIE KLAUSNER is the creator and co-star of Hulu's *Difficult People* and the host of the podcast *How Was Your Week*. She's a nice enough sort.

TREVOR KOSKI grew up in the Upper Peninsula of Michigan. He wrote these letters shortly after moving to San Francisco. They were his first published work. They were also his second-to-last published work. He still lives in San Francisco, now with his wife and their two children. He works at the City Attorney's Office. He has not seen Rabs in over twenty years.

SCAACHI KOUL is a senior culture writer at BuzzFeed News and the author of *One Day We'll All Be Dead and None of This Will Matter*. She lives in Brooklyn, but who doesn't.

R.O. KWON's nationally bestselling first novel, *The Incendiaries*, was published by Riverhead (U.S.) and Virago/Little Brown (UK) and is being translated into seven languages. Named a best book of the year by over forty publications, *The Incendiaries* received the Housatonic Book Award and was a finalist or nominated for seven other prizes, including the National Book Critics Circle John Leonard Award for Best First Book and *Los Angeles Times* First Book Prize. Kwon's writing has appeared in the *New York Times*, the *Guardian*, the *Paris Review*, NPR, and elsewhere.

JONATHAN LETHEM is the author of over twenty books of fiction and essays. His twelfth novel, *The Arrest*, was published in November 2020.

DAVID LIDA is the author of several books, including *First Stop in the New World: Mexico City, the Capital of the 21st Century*

(Riverhead) and *Las llaves de la ciudad: un mosaico de México* (Sexto Piso). When he is not writing, he works as an investigator for lawyers in the U.S. who defend Mexican nationals charged with capital murder, and who are as such facing the death penalty. This work is the point of departure for his novel *One Life* (Unnamed). His website address is www.davidlida.com.

ALI LIEBEGOTT is a painter and writer. Her books include *The Beautifully Worthless*, *The IHOP Papers*, *Cha-Ching!*, and *The Summer of Dead Birds*. She currently lives in Los Angeles and writes for television.

SARAH MANGUSO is the author of seven books including *300 Arguments*, *Ongoingness*, *The Guardians*, and *The Two Kinds of Decay*. She lives in Los Angeles.

ANTHONY MARRA is the author of *The Tsar of Love and Techno*, a finalist for the National Book Critics Circle Award, and *A Constellation of Vital Phenomena*, which was longlisted for the National Book Award.

INGRIDA MARTINKUS is an architect and writer based in Chicago, Illinois. She is the seventh most interesting woman in the world.

CARSON MELL lives in California with his wife and daughter. His latest novel, *Cherry on Top*, is available as an exclusive audio-book from Audible; you can buy the rest of his books at www.carsonmell.com.

JOHN MOE is a writer and podcaster in Saint Paul. His latest book is *The Hilarious World of Depression*.

AVERY MONSEN is an actor and writer who lives in Los Angeles. He's the illustrator and co-author of several books, including the national bestseller *All My Friends Are Dead*. His next one is *I Am the Longest Dog*, coming in 2021. More info at averymonsen.com.

LARAINE NEWMAN is a founding member of The Groundlings and original cast member of *Saturday Night Live*. She's worked for directors ranging from Woody Allen to Guillermo Del Toro. She is on the board of San Francisco Sketchfest, soon to celebrate twenty years. Her credits can be found on IMDB or at larainenewman.com.

THAO NGUYEN (of Thao & The Get Down Stay Down) is a songwriter, musician, and producer. She is based in the Bay Area. Her latest album, *Temple*, was released in May 2020 on Ribbon Music.

TOM O'DONNELL is an author and screenwriter living in Brooklyn, New York. His latest book series is called *Homerooms & Hall Passes*. He is not the president of the Teamsters Union.

JENNY ODELL is a multidisciplinary artist and writer based in Oakland, California. Her writing has appeared in the *New York Times*, *New York*, the *Atlantic*, the *Washington Post*, the *Believer*, the *Paris Review*, *McSweeney's*, SFMOMA's Open Space, the Creative Independent, and *Sierra Magazine*. Her bestselling book *How to Do Nothing: Resisting the Attention Economy* was published by Melville House in 2019.

NIELA ORR is a deputy editor of the *Believer*, a columnist at the *Baffler*, and a contributing editor of the *Organist* podcast. A 2019 Eleanor Kagi Foundation Writer-in-Residence at the

Black Mountain Institute, her writing has appeared in the *New York Times Book Review*, BuzzFeed, *Elle*, *Glamour*, *Harper's Bazaar*, and *McSweeney's Quarterly*.

ELENA PASSARELLO's essays have recently appeared in *National Geographic*, the *Paris Review*, and *Best American Science and Nature Writing*. She is the author of two award-winning collections, *Let Me Clear My Throat* and *Animals Strike Curious Poses*, the latter of which has been translated into four languages. She teaches in the MFA programs at Oregon State University and Vermont College of Fine Arts and can be heard weekly on the radio as a part of the PRX arts and culture show *LiveWire!*

KEATON PATTI is a writer and comedian living in New York City. He has contributed writings to the *New Yorker*, Marvel, Comedy Central, Netflix, and the *Onion*. He can also be found on the internet forcing a bot to write things. You may remember him from the previous sentences.

ANNA PERVUKHIN SAMMONS is a criminal defense lawyer. She lives in Eugene, Oregon.

JASON POLAN was an American artist born in Ann Arbor, Michigan, who lived and worked in New York City. Polan's illustrations have been published in the *New Yorker*, the *New York Times*, *Metropolis Magazine*, and *McSweeney's Quarterly Concern*, among others. He was the author of *Every Person in New York*.

BRENDAN EMMETT QUIGLEY has been a professional puzzle maker since 1996. When not weaving words, he plays a 1933 Royal in the Boston Typewriter Orchestra. Brendan lives in Brookline, Mass. with his wife, Liz, and their daughter, Tabitha.

SIMON RICH has written for *Saturday Night Live*, Pixar and *The Simpsons*. He is the creator of *Man Seeking Woman* (FXX) and *Miracle Workers* (TBS), which he based on his books. His latest collection, *Hits and Misses*, won the 2019 Thurber Prize for American Humor.

MIKE SACKS works for *Vanity Fair* and contributes humor to the *New Yorker*, *Time*, *Esquire*, *GQ*, the *Believer*, *Vice*, *Salon*, *McSweeney's*, the *New York Times*, the *Washington Post*, and other publications. He is the author of eight books and three audio projects.

ELIZABETH SANKEY is a writer, musician and filmmaker from London. In 2019 she released her directorial debut *Romantic Comedy*, a feature documentary about the genre, which screened at many festivals around the world including SXSW, IFFR, Sheffield Doc/Fest, and AFI Fest. It was distributed by Mubi in the UK and 1091 in North America. As a cultural commentator, she has written for the *Guardian*, *NME*, *Vice*, and *LOVE* magazine. With her band Summer Camp she has released four studio albums on Moshi Moshi.

SLOAN SCHANG is a digital strategist in Portland, Oregon who frequently writes for the internet. A parenting book is in the works, based loosely on his adventures with two young kids exploring the wilds of the Pacific Northwest.

JENNY SHANK's novel *The Ringer* won the High Plains Book Award. Her stories, essays, satire, and reviews have appeared in the *Atlantic*, the *Washington Post*, the *Guardian*, *Prairie Schooner*, *Alaska Quarterly Review*, *Michigan Quarterly Review*, the Toast, and *Barrelhouse*. Her work has been honorably mentioned by

The Best American Essays, the Pushcart Prize anthology, and her mother. She teaches in the Mile High MFA program at Regis University and the Lighthouse Writers Workshop in Denver.

JIM STALLARD grew up in Missouri and is now a science writer in New York City. He has contributed more than forty pieces to McSweeney's Internet Tendency since 2000.

JEN STATSKY is an Emmy-nominated writer and producer. Her credits include *The Good Place*, *Broad City*, and *Parks and Recreation*. She is currently based in Los Angeles, California.

DON STEINBERG writes for the *Wall Street Journal* and sometimes the *New Yorker* and publishes a humor zine called *Meanwhile*. He also co-hosts the podcast *Vegan Sympathizer*.

YUKIKO TAKEUCHI lives and works in Atlanta, Georgia, where she is twenty years older than when she wrote the letter in this book and no longer peppers the internet with her musings.

MICHELLE TEA is the author of over a dozen books for adults, kids, and teenagers. She is the creator of Drag Queen Story Hour. She lives in Los Angeles with her kid and her cat.

RUFI THORPE grew up in southern California, whose people and coastlines and real estate listings continue to obsess her. After college, she spent some time as a waitress at a poorly run French café before being accepted as a Henry Hoyns Fellow at the University of Virginia's MFA program, where she learned to fish and wrote two novels that were not very good. Years of incredibly depressing waitressing followed before she sold her first novel, *The Girls from Corona del Mar*, which was longlisted for the Dylan Thomas and Flaherty-Dunnan First Novel Prize. Thorpe's latest novel, *The Knockout Queen*, published in April 2020, was an IndieNext Pick and a Book of the Month. She lives with her husband, two sons, and insane dog in Los Angeles.

AVERY TRUFELMAN is an audio writer and essayist who hosts podcast series for *99% Invisible* and *Curbed*.

NOVUYO ROSA TSHUMA is a 2020 Lannan Fiction Fellow and the author of the critically acclaimed novel *House of Stone*. A native of Zimbabwe who has lived in South Africa and the United States, she serves on the editorial advisory board and is an editor at the *Bare Life Review*, a journal of refugee and immigrant literature based in San Francisco. She has taught fiction at the Iowa Writers' Workshop, and serves as an assistant professor of fiction at Emerson College.

DEB OLIN UNFERTH is the author of six books, including, most recently, the novel *Barn 8*.

SARAH VOWELL is a journalist and the author of seven nonfiction books on American history and culture including *Lafayette in the Somewhat United States*.

STUART WADE is a writer and consultant in Austin, Texas.

TEDDY WAYNE is the author of the novels *Apartment*, *Loner*, *The Love Song of Jonny Valentine*, and *Kapitoil*. He is the winner of a Whiting Writers' Award and an NEA Creative Writing Fellowship as well as a finalist for the Young Lions Fiction Award, PEN/Bingham Prize, and Dayton Literary Peace Prize. A regular contributor to the *New York Times*, the *New Yorker*, and *McSweeney's*, he has taught at Columbia University and Washington University in St. Louis.

COLLEEN WERTHMANN is an Emmy-losing comedy writer and actor whose credits include *The Daily Show with Trevor Noah*, *The Nightly Show with Larry Wilmore*, and the Academy Awards. She's the showrunner on Laura Bell Bundy's upcoming sketch/variety show about women's history, and teaches/mentors with Sundance Institute and Writers Guild Initiative. Colleen has also been a mid-level theater actor, an international civil servant, and a fetus.

COLIN WINNETTE is the author of several books, including *The Job of the Wasp* (Soft Skull Press), *Haints Stay* (Two Dollar Radio), and *Coyote* (winner of Les Figues Press's NOS Book Contest). His writing has appeared in numerous journals and anthologies, but this was his first letter to the editor.

KENT WOODYARD is the author of *Nonessential Mnemonics: An Unnecessary Journey into Senseless Knowledge* and the co-host of *The Dream Job Podcast* (thedreamjobpodcast.com). Depending on when you're reading this, he is either working for a large tech company that you've heard of or for a less large tech company that you haven't. He and his wife live outside Seattle with their two children.

The editor is grateful to Claire Boyle, Eric Cromie, Alia DeBurro, Madison Decter, Annie Dills, Kitania Folk, Alexandra Galou, Chris Monks, Paz O'Farrell, Raj Tawney, Sunra Thompson, Amanda Uhle, and Dan Weiss for their generous assistance.